DR BOB WOODWAR
United Kingdom. Having
schools, he became a co-worker at the Sheiling School in Thornbury, a centre of the Camphill Community, based on the teachings of Rudolf Steiner (1861-1925). He remained within the Camphill Movement, living with and teaching children with special educational needs, for some forty years, retiring in 2012. He took a special interest in understanding autism in children and young people.

At the age of 46, Bob received an M.Ed degree from Bristol University, followed by an M.Phil at the age of 50 and a Ph.D from the University of the West of England at the age of 64. As well as being a qualified educator, he is a spiritual healer and the author of several books. He has been married for forty-two years and has five grown-up children and many grandchildren.

By the same author:

Spirit Healing (2004)
Spirit Communications (2007)
Spiritual Healing with Children with Special Needs (2007)
Trusting in Spirit – The Challenge (2018)

Autism – A Holistic Approach (with Dr Marga Hogenboom)
(3rd edition, 2013)

KNOWLEDGE OF SPIRIT WORLDS AND LIFE AFTER DEATH

As received through spirit guides

Dr Bob Woodward

The author encourages readers to make their own choices and decisions in relation to the contents of this book. Any advice, recommendations or teachings given herein should be subject to individual judgement.

Clairview Books Ltd.,
Russet, Sandy Lane,
West Hoathly,
W. Sussex RH19 4QQ

www.clairviewbooks.com

Published by Clairview Books 2020

A CIP catalogue record for this book is available from the British Library

ISBN 978 1 912992 16 4

Cover by Morgan Creative
Typeset by Symbiosys Technologies, Vishakapatnam, India
Printed and bound by 4Edge Ltd, Essex

Contents

Dedication	vi
Acknowledgements	vii
Foreword by Peter John	1
1. Introduction	2
2. Analogy	8
3. Insights	12
4. Spirit Guides	19
5. After Death	33
6. Spirit Worlds	47
7. Where We Live There	68
8. Family, Friends, Pets	76
9. What We Do There	87
Addendum: Climate Changes?	99
10. How Long?	103
11. Reincarnation	114
12. Before Birth	128
Appendix: Conversations with my Father in the Afterlife	137
Afterword	151
Bibliography	154
About the Author	156

Dedication

To my good friend Carter Nelson who passed into spirit on 13 May 2018 while this book was being written. We first met, in our mid-twenties, as students at Emerson College in Sussex. Thereafter I continued my career in special needs education in the Camphill movement, whilst Carter found his place teaching in mainstream Steiner school education. From time to time we saw each other briefly. However, it was in the last years of Carter's life, through illness, that we came together regularly and shared in lively conversations. These were always peppered with a good dose of humour, mainly directed towards our own shortcomings as fellow seekers on the anthroposophical path of knowledge. I sincerely hope Carter approves of this latest book, as he did of its predecessor also given from my spirit guides.

Acknowledgements

I am grateful for the encouragement to write this book given me by my good friends, Anne Lewis, Pete Newberry ('Peter John') and Neil Castleton. However, even with their welcome support nothing would have been forthcoming without the active cooperation of my friends in spirit, namely the eight guides with whom I conversed. I simply acted as the enquirer, and willing recipient, for the knowledge of spirit worlds that they communicated to us. Many thanks also to Hazel Townsley who, once again, transformed my untidy script into crystal clear print. For then also providing me with honest and helpful feedback on the completed manuscript, my sincere thanks to Michael Luxford, Terry Maley, Charlotte DeLotz, Erhard Keller and Graham Rickett. My gratitude also to Sevak Gulbekian and the team at Clairview Books for their willingness to publish this work.

Finally, I thank my father for his contributions as given in the Appendix. Although a late addition, the Appendix could just as well be read as a fitting Prologue for this enquiry. This quite new thought actually came to me on the twenty-fifth anniversary of his death.

Foreword

I have been a Psychic Artist since 1986 and have been an enthusiast in drawing spirit guides for people ever since. I met Bob about five years ago in Chipping Sodbury in South Gloucestershire in the UK. I gave him a reading and drew him a spirit guide. We talked at length about the authenticity of communicating with spirit guides and found we had much in common on the subject.

Bob is passionate about his work. His knowledge goes back to his youth and experiences gained through the study of teachings by the Austrian spiritual researcher, Rudolf Steiner.

This book brings an in-depth look at life in the spirit world either after death or before we are born into this world.

Bob shows a confidence in his own ability to make not only a relevant connection with these 'salient beings' but to interpret the answers they give to his questions with honesty and clarity.

This style enables the reader to want to follow Bob's questioning and show a thirst for more.

Everyone with a curiosity for spiritual knowledge should read this excellent book.

Peter John
Andover, Hampshire, UK

1
Introduction

I began writing this Introduction in May 2018 when not yet three weeks had elapsed since the publication of my last book, *Trusting in Spirit – The Challenge*. This was therefore a very quick follow on, to say the least! However, at the end of that book I wrote that,

> A third book, still to be written, will aim to bring through knowledge of the spirit worlds *per se* as given by the guides. It will hopefully answer some of the many questions which people, who are open to the idea of an afterlife, may have.

The aim and intention of this new book, as a sequel to the last one, was therefore very clear to me. Namely to do further original research together with my spirit guides, in order to throw light on the nature and characteristics of those dimensions which are hidden from our ordinary sense perceptions. What was not yet at all clear, however, was exactly how this intention would be realised, and what form and contents this current book might have. Although this was then really a complete mystery to me, I did already have the assurance from the eight spirit guides who figured in *Trusting in Spirit – The Challenge* that they were very willing to cooperate with me again. Indeed, without their inputs and help, the new project would simply not be possible at all. I felt that they were the ones who were best placed to help enlighten us about what life is like in spirit worlds.

After a good deal of study and thought it is my conviction that we have, in fact, all lived in these higher worlds before being born on Earth, and also that we shall pass into these same worlds after our physical deaths. In a very real sense these higher, spirit worlds, are actually our true homeland, whereas our physical, material, existence is but our temporary abode here and now. Of this belief, or assumption, the rational materialist may immediately react with scorn and scepticism, claiming that it is simply not evidence-based. This is a viewpoint that I can well understand, for we live in a time when seeing is believing and hard, scientific, so-called objective evidence must take precedence over any subjective beliefs, dogmas or superstitions. I can also understand,

and agree with, those who assert that any knowledge claims should be properly tested to ascertain their credibility, reliability and validity. Of course, what exactly counts as genuine knowledge or what the process of knowing actually entails is a rather complex subject in its own epistemological right. Indeed the moment we start to delve behind the seeming realities of everyday, sense-perceptible existence, the ground on which we ordinarily stand may become very shaky! The theory and findings of quantum mechanics, for example, leads us into a very different scenario from the one we naively assume as real and solid, including our own material bodies. However, this present book is not intended to be either scientific or philosophic in any intellectually rigorous or theoretical sense. Far rather it is largely experiential, qualitative and empirical in nature, being based on my trust in my spirit guides to communicate with me telepathically. This is an ongoing process that began more than fourteen years ago and is charted in my two previous books, *Spirit Communications* (2007) and *Trusting in Spirit – The Challenge* (2018).

Now, I am not asking anyone to simply believe what will be written in these pages since I passionately believe that everyone should be left free to make up their own minds and reach their own conclusions about such matters. Nonetheless, the subject of this book surely concerns us all, provided of course that we do at least consider the real possibility that death is not the finale for us, once and for all. If you do however think that it is the unequivocal end of your existence as a distinct being, then this book is probably irrelevant to you. That is, unless you are at least open to read it, think about it, and then reassess your viewpoint in the light of it. However that may be, clearly no one can dispute the fact that we are all born into this earthly world at various points of time and that, at other points of time, we will inevitably meet our mortal deaths. Where exactly we have originally come from and where we might go to, beyond the physical boundaries of birth and death, are perennial questions which have probably occupied human beings for millennia. If we are fully satisfied with the answers which modern biology gives us, then we may perhaps rest easy in the belief that our cells, genes and chromosomes are the bedrock and legacy of our cosmic existence. Any notion of the continuation of our life essence beyond death must then be looked for only in the common genetic pool of humanity. Our mind, our thoughts, feelings, emotions, intentions and all else that is encompassed in our personality, including any sense of our own uniqueness, may be seen simply as a temporary creation of our complex brain chemistry. Or can it?

If this purely materialistic perspective does not fully satisfy us, does not somehow live up to our expectations as thinking, feeling, willing beings, then we may be open to consider alternative explanations for our rich inner life, our comings and goings and our whys and wherefores. While we can certainly admire the exact methods, intricate theories, and spectacular technical achievements of the hard-sciences, in comparison our real lives are often very messy, convoluted, stressful and inexact. They are of course also at times very joyful, exhilarating, liberating and peaceful, as well as sometimes thoroughly depressing and boring! In the kaleidoscopic vagaries of our lived-experiences the rigours of, say, theoretical physics, that inspired such an intellectual luminary as the late Professor Stephen Hawking, do not really feature as something very important or relevant to most of us. However interesting, perhaps even fascinating, they are of very limited use in terms of our daily lives. On the other hand, Professor Hawking's obvious courage, tenacity, determination, humour and humanity do immediately resonate with us as qualities that very much matter in everyday life! We might perhaps value, together with these positive attributes, also notions of spirituality, transcendence, and meaningfulness which do not necessarily need to be rooted in any particular faiths, creeds, traditions or dogmas. Such themes as these clearly do belong in the context of this present book, which is based on the central premise that there really *is* an innate spirituality lying deep within us, as the very core and meaning of our being. Moreover, that this transcendent spirituality is related to, and linked with, other dimensions within our universe, which we may refer to as higher or spirit worlds. It is to begin to explore, understand and investigate these other worlds that this book has been written. Thereby we may learn to experience a greater sense of connectedness and belonging than we might otherwise have. It could of course be argued that we already have all the connectedness we need right here in our busy daily lives, without imagining any further, higher dimensions to our existence. After all, our mobile phones and the worldwide web give us ready access to global communications and information.

True though this is, how greatly we can feel the loss when death appears to dramatically sever our close links with family or friends. How painfully empty and lonely our lives may then become, compared to the companionship and love we once shared. Modern technology, for all its benefits, is of little or no avail to us in terms of recompense for our very personal loss. However, what if it is actually possible to maintain a genuine living connection with our deceased loved ones, and what if we each have spirit guides as invisible friends who want to help us, from out of their non-material dimensions? Then does it not make sense to turn towards them, both relatives and guides, in order to try to strike up a conscious rapport with them? Certainly it has become my own direct lived-experience that spirit guides in particular can help us to consider that we live within a spiritual, multi-dimensional universe as well as a physical one. To at least be open to such possibilities is the attitude of mind and heart on which the main contents of this book must stand. Those contents will take the form of conversations on interrelated themes which I have had with the guides who have cooperated in bringing this book about. However, I will also supplement each chapter with a short commentary on what the guides have said and, in doing so, refer especially to the research findings given by the Austrian philosopher and spiritual-scientist Rudolf Steiner. The reason that I base my commentaries largely on the work of Steiner is not only because of the great extent and depth of his spiritual investigations, but most importantly because of his fully-conscious clairvoyant methodology. Indeed, Steiner emphasised the need for such conscious research methods in contrast to any trance-like or somnambulant techniques for accessing psychic or spiritual information. Will the commentaries show some clear validation and agreement with what the guides have communicated to us, or will definite contrasts and divergencies emerge? At this stage in the book, neither you nor I know how this will be, but it will certainly be very interesting to find out! It is one way at least of trying to compare and assess what I have received uniquely from my guides, by reference to other independent research findings.

For students of Steiner's anthroposophy, or spiritual science, there is no shortage of literature available. His written books and the transcripts of his 6,000 or so lectures are collected together in hundreds of volumes and cover a wide range of subjects. I will however particularly refer to some of those sources in which Steiner described 'the journey' which we will undergo between our death and our new birth on Earth. Such accounts usually give the big, general picture of what befalls us and, therefore, lack the more specific and individualised scenarios. To obtain the latter, it would probably be necessary to follow a particular soul on their unique pathway after death (see Appendix).

Rudolf Steiner did not regard anthroposophy as a system of philosophy but as a spiritual science *per se*, especially in respect of its methodology as 'a path of knowledge' of the human being and the cosmos.

Although Steiner also produced philosophical works, these preceded his actual anthroposophical researches and findings.

As I pointed out previously in my book *Trusting in Spirit – The Challenge,* it seems always important to me to do all we can to check the accuracy, reliability and validity of what has been given by our guides. Spirit guides are not, I believe, either omniscient or infallible and neither is our own ability to always receive their communications correctly. In this field of spiritual research we need to be as truthful, honest and thorough as we can. This is certainly my aim and I must leave it to you as thoughtful readers to judge to what extent I have achieved this. You may of course – indeed you must – ask the question, 'How do we know that what is contained in this book is true, or has any truth in it?' even if there appears to be good correlation between the contents of the conversations and the commentaries. Also, of course, bearing in mind my own possible biases in composing the commentaries, say in support of my guides. My answer to that question is, 'Probably, you don't!' But I would also say, 'How do you actually know that anything, in any book, is really true?' What indeed is truth, as opposed to faith or fiction or belief or assumption? Well, here it all rather depends, I think, on what level we are looking for the truth. If I want to know the truth about how my car is designed and how it works, then I can consult the maker's handbook. On this, mechanical, level I can be very confident that I can find out the truths about my car. If on the other hand I want to find out the truths about the construction, design and functioning of our universe, then the situation is much more complicated. It may be well beyond my human grasp – indeed, perhaps, beyond any human's comprehension, even including the late Professor Hawking.

Clearly the question of knowing whether something is really true or not is more or less easy to answer, depending on exactly what subject area, or domain, we're talking about. With cars, washing machines, fridges, it is comparatively easy; with universes, different states of consciousness and possible spirit worlds, it is relatively difficult. With the latter examples, we may have to treat any descriptions or explanations we receive at first as working hypotheses or paradigms. However, as the evidence increases and our confidence grows, these hypotheses may become theories that seem increasingly credible and believable. It may then come to the point where an established theory, let us say of Darwinian Evolution, more or less assumes the status of a sure fact, or the truth – at least until some other facts are discovered, which may then necessitate a new working hypothesis or theory!

However, we also need to bear in mind that spiritual research is based on inwardly perceived phenomena, rather than on any outer sense impressions. Steiner claims that he does not formulate hypotheses, but rather reports his own direct experiences and perceptions of spiritual dimensions, beings and events.

Given the challenges for gaining true insights, what is it then that drives us forward with all our ceaseless searching and seeking for answers? In part it is our curiosity, ignorance and fears! We seek always for some greater reassurance and certainty in life through better understanding and knowledge. It is even said that, 'The Truth shall make you free'. Free of what? Fear, uncertainty, insecurity, anxiety and ignorance. Therefore, although it is also said, 'To err is human', we continually try to get it right and sort out truth from fiction. The scientific way to do this is through the qualitative and quantitative methods of serious research. All research starts with at least one question and that root question may rapidly lead to many others. And so we go on the quest to discover answers, credible solutions, which we try to validate in various ways, such as by doing experiments and investigations which can be replicated and the results compared. Now, the main themes in this book are deliberately put in the form of questions – 'research questions', we can say. These I will put to and discuss with the spirit guides who are cooperating with me. I will also describe the methodology of exactly how I go about this form of spirit communication.

So, when the guides have given their answers to the questions will we then know something of the truth of these topics? I sincerely hope we will and that, I suggest, is the very best that we can do in this one book. Research is of course an ongoing process, and further questions and investigations, and perhaps comparisons, may shed still greater light on the themes which we will turn to from Chapter 4 onwards. If, as my guides tell me, we each have a repository of wisdom, of truth, deep in our own hearts, then perhaps if we learn to become still and feel what lives there, we might find inner confirmation of our true nature and of spirit worlds – those worlds which, I strongly believe, we are really part of here and now, as well as in the hereafter.

This book is intended to be easily accessible for all who are searching for answers to the themes which it addresses, and I hope this proves to be the case for the widest possible readership. Let us now set the stage for our cooperative inquiry.

2
Analogy

When, just the other day, I asked an old friend of mine, now in his hundredth year, whom I visit in his nursing home, 'Why might it be important that we know something about the spiritual world before we die?', he thought for a while. Then he replied that a certain lady he knew had said that, 'So we might feel more at home when we pass over there'. This lady was, apparently, the wife of a priest. I think this was a pretty good answer to my question. If we consider that death is the doorway from this familiar earthly world to the 'next world' where, instead of our extinction, we begin to live some form of afterlife, then it makes perfect sense to try to learn something about this place before we actually go there.

Already as a youth, perhaps even as a child, I asked myself the question, 'What happens to us when we die?' Some of my friends thought it quite strange, perhaps even morbid, that I would wonder about such things as a young person, but nonetheless I did. In fact, I even sometimes imagined what it would be like if I could look down, so to speak, at my own funeral and see the reactions of those present! As well, and also from a young age, I sometimes wondered what was the greater reality, my own dreams or the outer physical world? Yet another recurrent question arose for me when I puzzled about my own inner life of thoughts and images. 'Where', I asked, 'do my thoughts come from, and especially those that just seem to appear in my mind from out of nowhere?' Perhaps my interest, in my later teens, in studying philosophy was inspired by my naturally reflective and introspective turn of mind. So, from these more personal observations let us now return to the central question of whether we can learn something of spirit worlds, so that we can feel more at home there when, perhaps, one day we transition to them. What is required for us to gain foreknowledge of this new land, if indeed we can? Let us explore this question via an analogy.

If we were going to set out on a journey to some remote foreign country, it would no doubt make a lot of sense to find out all that we could about it in advance. Moreover, the route we would choose to take, as well as the final destination itself, would warrant our careful preparations and considerations. Not that we could know *everything* beforehand because this would be anyway impossible and nor, in all probability, would we want to forfeit the freshness and novelty of the adventure. Even if we had heard accounts of where we were heading, or even saw images of this, say in a film or TV travel programme, we would be looking forward to having our own unique experiences; our very own 'take' on what was there for us to see, feel, touch, hear, taste, smell, etc. Nothing can really replace, or better, our own direct personal perceptions of the realities into which we decide to plunge or immerse ourselves. Nonetheless, due preparation is important for a whole host of reasons, including our personal safety and wellbeing. So, let us continue further with this analogy of making a journey to a foreign land, *vis-à-vis* our wish to learn something of spirit worlds before the day of our inevitable departure, which might perhaps be sooner than we expect!

As regards places to visit on our planet, we are surely spoilt for choice. Even seasoned world-travellers would readily admit that there are still countless destinations which they have not yet explored. In this sense we can liken our quest to that of the first pioneers who set forth on their journeys, by land or sea, not knowing what they might encounter along the way. Indeed in those early days, when they sailed east or west, they knew not whether they would simply fall off the edge of the world at the far horizon! Depending on your point of view, these bold adventurers were either extremely courageous or quite mad, to venture from their familiar comfort zones. The moment we contemplate undertaking our own modest journeys of discovery, many relevant questions spring to mind. Moreover the whole undertaking has added dimensions if we intend not simply to make a short visit to that foreign land, but wish to stay there for a longer time and perhaps even make our new home there. In that case we would probably find it even more important to gather as much practical information as we could about this new place. Such information could include what the terrain is like – say, deserts, forests, plains, mountains, lakes, etc. – what sort of climate and weather to expect, the biodiversity of the country with its flora and fauna and other inhabitants, and the culture, customs and laws of the land. The more we can learn prior to our departure from our well-known familiar setting, the better prepared we shall be to acclimatise, adapt and feel at home in our new surroundings. In particular, of course, to make friends and be happy there, for on this will largely depend our quality of life, our inner security and feelings of well-being. Clearly we hope that our move will be a great success and not turn out to be a disappointment or a disaster!

At this point then let us draw this scenario, this analogy, to a close and remind ourselves what this book is really about. It is intended to be an informative guide-book, not for any earthly destination, but to enlighten us about those spirit worlds that we may very well be passing into after our physical deaths. It is therefore not meant as an intellectual exercise or as a fantasy, but as a serious enquiry of vital interest to many of us, certainly to those who are not convinced that death marks our total annihilation and dissolution. If there really is such a thing as an afterlife, then what is it like and what can we expect from it? Many of us will already know of family members and friends who have gone before us, gone, that is, through the gate of death. If somehow they still exist as individuals, where are they now? Are they happy? What sort of world do they inhabit? Do we have any good means of knowing this, of finding out how they are faring? These are far from abstract questions, but may very well be of the greatest importance for the quality and happiness of our own lives whilst still living on Earth, particularly so, if we have lost loved ones prematurely in traumatic or tragic circumstances, rather than simply through ripe old age. Depending perhaps on our religious beliefs and assumptions, we may wonder if there really is a heaven and a hell and, if there is, what determines our personal fates after death?

In his second book, *The Map of Heaven*, the neurosurgeon Dr Eben Alexander explores the mysteries of the afterlife. His views are based on his own profound near-death experiences, and also those of others. In Chapter 6 he writes,

> There are trees in the worlds above this one. There are fields, and there are animals and people. There is water, too – water in abundance. It flows in rivers and descends as rain. Mists arise from the pulsing surfaces of these waters, and fish glide beneath them. Not abstract, mathematical fish, either. Real ones. Every bit as real as any fish you've seen, and way, way more so. The waters there are like earthly water. And yet they're not earthly water. They are, to state it in a way that I know falls short but is accurate all the same, more than simply earthly water. It's water that is closer to the source. Closer, like the water higher up on a meandering river is closer to the springs from which it emerges. It's water that's deeply familiar – so that when you see it you realise that all the most beautiful waterscapes you ever saw on earth were beautiful

> precisely because they were reminding you of it. It's living water, the way everything is living up there, and it pulls you in, so that your gaze wants to travel into it, deeper and deeper, on and on, forever. It was water that made all the earthly bodies of water I've seen, from Carolina beaches to western rivers, seem like lesser versions, little siblings of this, the thing that on some deep level I'd always known water should be.
>
> That's not to denigrate the oceans and rivers and lakes and thunderstorms and all the other forms of water I've seen and enjoyed on this earth. It is, instead, simply to say that I now see these waters in a new perspective, just as I see all of the natural beauties of the earth in a similarly new one. When we ascend, in short, everything's still there. Only it's more real. Less dense, yet at the same time more intense – more there. The objects and landscapes and people and animals burst with life and colour. The world above is as vast and various and populated and as different in one place than in another as this one is, and infinitely more so.
>
> (Alexander, 2014. pp.92-93)

Well, is he correct in these almost homely descriptions? How reliable are they actually? Are NDEs sufficient, in their spontaneous methodology, to give us a full and comprehensive insight into the reality of spirit worlds? At this stage in our enquiry we clearly have many more questions than answers but, of these, the most pressing question must surely be, 'Can we obtain reliable information, real knowledge of spirit worlds, if they do actually exist?' We want to gain true insights into these regions so that we can form a picture, a concrete, tangible picture, not an airy-fairy one, of what we shall be stepping into ourselves, sooner or later. So what possible means, methods, resources, are available to us in this endeavour, in this knowledge-quest? This is the theme we will turn to in the next chapter.

3
Insights

When asking the question, 'How can we gain insights and knowledge of higher, spirit worlds beyond the physical?', we can just briefly return to our earlier analogy. Namely, our preparations to visit some foreign land. If, let's say, we want to go to China for the first time in our lives, then we can turn to various sources of information. These can include books about the country with large-scale and more local maps; perhaps a guide to the language and to various social mores, and also the common laws of the land. We can learn something as well of the history and typical traditions of Chinese culture. Information could also include particular places of interest, where best to stay, to eat out, things to do (and not to do), means of transport, currency, and so on. However, if reading books does not much appeal to us, then perhaps we can watch relevant travel programmes on the TV or internet, or get an informative tourist DVD. We might also listen to CDs of Chinese music, speech, poetry, or visit an art gallery with examples of Chinese painting, porcelain and sculptures. All this prior knowledge will greatly serve to help us build up a colourful, multi-dimensional picture of China before we arrive there. However, another very good way of gaining insights would be to actually speak with people who are living in China now, and who are able to communicate clearly to us in our own language. One great advantage of dialogue with real people is that we could then ask various questions which arise for us in the course of our conversations. Although books, films and CDs can teach us much, the personal contact with others can feel much more alive, vibrant and to the point. Perhaps these same people can also meet and welcome us and show us around when we arrive.

The relevance of our foreign travel analogy, and especially the direct contact with real people living in China, becomes clearer when we now consider the various ways in which we can try to gain some knowledge of spirit worlds. Naturally any such knowledge-claims will need to be tested and examined carefully in order to ascertain their credibility, reliability and validity. The ways by which we may do this will be considered a little later. Sources of possible insights into spirit worlds may include the following literature: accounts of near-death experiences

(NDEs) and out-of-body experiences (OBEs); spiritual and religious traditions; specific esoteric literature; and books written by mediums, psychics, clairvoyants and channellers. An in-depth study and comparison of some of these published sources may enable us to come to a coherent picture and understanding of the alleged nature and characteristics of spirit worlds and of our relationship with them. However, to conduct a thorough comparative and perhaps rather academic study is beyond the remit of this current book, given that it is largely experiential in nature. Nonetheless, and as I have already stated, an important resource for me are the many books and lectures given by the spiritual researcher Rudolf Steiner (1861-1925). I have been a student of Steiner's work, known as anthroposophy, for the past fifty years and this has therefore been a major influence in my own life, my world-view and beliefs. I say 'beliefs' because although Steiner himself was clearly convinced about the veracity of his research, I cannot claim to have my own direct clairvoyant experiences of what he described, for example, of the various regions or levels of the soul and spirit worlds given in his book *Theosophy*, or of his account of the spiritual evolution of the world presented in his *An Outline of Esoteric Science*. Steiner wrote these seminal books during the first quarter of the twentieth century, over one hundred years ago, and it has to be said that both the contents and the style of his published works may possibly not appeal to many people nowadays. Particularly so in the light of such a current wealth of popular and accessible spirituality literature, which has its roots in the New Age movements of the 1960s and '70s. There are many books on angels, spirit guides, the human aura, chakra energy-centres, nature spirits, near-death experiences, psychic adventures, etc. Very importantly, however, Steiner provides us early on in his work with thorough descriptions of safe and sound methods whereby to achieve a knowledge of higher worlds. Indeed, in 1909 he published in German the book which is entitled in English, *Knowledge of the Higher Worlds – How is it Achieved?* This volume is still in print and has been re-translated and revised numerous times. It remains an open question whether, since its first publication, any of his pupils have sufficiently developed their own clairvoyant faculties to independently validate Steiner's many research findings. Fortunately there are also other means available for us to 'test out', as it were, the results of Steiner's spiritual investigations. For example, anthroposophy has proven to be remarkably fruitful in terms of its many practical applications in a wide range of activities which include biodynamic agriculture, anthroposophic medicine, Steiner (Waldorf) education and social renewal. If it is found that in practice Steiner's ideas do work well, then this certainly increases the credibility for his underlying clairvoyant findings.

Now, the purpose of this present book is clearly not to make out a case for Steiner's anthroposophy or spiritual science *per se*, but instead to provide us with knowledge of spirit worlds as given by my guides. Since my aim is to present this in a form which is easily accessible and of interest to the widest possible audience, hopefully the conversational format of the next chapters will help readers feel to be actual participants in these various enquiries. If then the knowledge provided by the guides is also largely corroborated by what Rudolf Steiner and perhaps others have given us, then this is all to the good. Although it appears that Steiner was able to leave his body consciously, in order to pursue his clairvoyant investigations of spirit worlds, I for one do not have this same ability! What I believe I can do, however, is to communicate telepathically with those already in spirit who are working with me on the contents of this book. My trust in this process of thought-communication has gradually emerged over the course of the past years and is well described in my two previous books. Since I cannot assume that you have read these earlier publications it is good to refer briefly to them here, in order that the contents of the chapters which follow can be viewed in the correct light. I am, however, not asking anyone to simply believe what has been communicated to me in this way. Rather, I ask you to give it your due consideration and thought. It rests firmly on the premise that spirit guides do actually exist, and that they are very willing to be of support to us in our earthly lives. Moreover, that they are also able to enlighten us about the dimensions which they inhabit in spirit, whereto we will also travel someday. In that sense our earlier analogy with speaking directly with friends living in China about their country and customs before we journey there is, I think, very apt.

My awareness of my two main spirit guides came about initially through my contact with Anne Lewis, a spiritual medium, in 2005. I wrote to Anne in December 2004 to request a postal reading from her, mainly to see if I would gain confirmation of my abilities as a spiritual healer. In the reading which I then received in January it was at once made clear that a spirit doctor was working with me in healing, and had been doing so already for some years. I know him as Dr John. I continued to ask Anne for regular readings, and in the fourth of these she made me aware of another guide who was linked with me. I know him as Joshua Isaiah. Whereas John is there for the spiritual healing work, Joshua is there to give teachings on spirit matters, philosophy and also for advice. As described in my book *Spirit Communications*, following John's suggestion to me to practise 'sitting in the silence', I then became able to clearly distinguish my own thoughts from those given to me telepathically from either him or Joshua. In this way it became possible to establish conscious two-way communication and gradually to strengthen my trust in the authenticity of this process. Indeed, I discovered that I was also able to communicate with others in spirit with this same methodology, including my deceased parents and my niece's son who died aged eleven in 2006.

For nearly fifteen years I have had regular contact and communication with John and Joshua, and this remains ongoing. However, in November 2016 I first became aware of another guide, called Markos, via a reading I had with the psychic artist Peter John. Sometime later, in March 2017, I also became aware of Red Cloud as another of my guides. As I have described in my book, *Trusting in Spirit – The Challenge*, in the course of 2017 yet other guides made themselves known to me. Therein are contained the teachings which I received from these eight distinct spirit guides, which includes Philip as my guardian angel and Pan as the Lord of Nature. (They each give their own introductions to readers in Chapter 3 of that book.) Indeed, I had the clear impression that this circle of guides had formed around me precisely in order to be able to make their contributions to the book I intended to write (and did so in the Summer of 2017). My way, or method, of communicating with these guides was exactly the same as I had already established with Dr John and Joshua, namely through conscious mental telepathy. I emphasised in Chapter 2 of *Trusting in Spirit – The Challenge*, when discussing my methodology, that I do not enter into any sort of trance condition, nor do I practise any special forms of breathing, posture or meditation when conversing with spirit sources. Neither do I engage in any form of so-called 'automatic writing' in order to put on paper what I receive from the guides. Instead I write down the thoughts which come to me in full, awake, consciousness. Although Dr John had originally suggested that I learn to 'sit in the silence' in order to be receptive to receiving his communications, this is no longer necessary. Whenever I wish to speak with any of the guides I simply turn my attention towards them, in the same way as I would in talking with any physical person. It really is as simple as that. You could say that to properly converse with anyone, we need to be able to tune in with them, to listen and to be on their frequency and wavelength. This is also how I see the inner process for conscious telepathic contact with friends in spirit.

Often, so-called 'channelled' communications with spirit take place with the medium in a state of trance in which he or she is unaware of what is being given through them. It is a lowered, rather than a heightened, condition of consciousness, certainly as regards their own self-awareness. This is not the mental state, nor methodology, in which I receive communications from my guides.

So, just to reiterate this process so that there is complete transparency about what I do, it is as follows. To engage in this form of communication there is always a clear intentionality and purpose for it, for example, to ask for advice on some matter, or to enquire if the guide has some particular teaching to impart. I then make myself inwardly receptive, still and open, adopt an inner listening attitude, become attentive, and then clearly distinguish my own thoughts from those that I receive telepathically. Often I will ask a specific guide to respond to my questions but, otherwise, I will be open for whichever guide chooses to step forward. In the latter case I go with which name first comes to my mind. This is the way in which most of the conversations in this book have emerged and is therefore a purely inner process and dialogue, until I record it in writing to share with others. However, when I go for a walk by myself and choose to converse with a guide, I usually speak out the answers verbally. Once this method has been established, it is easy to replicate at any time or place. Importantly there is never any imposition, coercion or demands made either by spirit entities or myself. On the contrary, it is a free and cooperative exchange, an open conversation which takes place between myself and my guides. However, the initiative for such conversations always comes from me.

My aim in 2017 was to receive the 'teachings' which the guides considered relevant and important to share with us at that time. When I had received all these from each guide in turn, I then had a 'question and answer' session also with each of them. Sometimes I challenged what they had said, and wanted readers to be left quite free to reflect on these dialogues for themselves. Though it was not my intention to try to convince anyone of the truth of the teachings, they were clearly intended to enlighten us in the down-to-earth challenges of our lives. It was made clear that spirit guides are very willing to be of help to us if we ask them to, but that they will never impose their will over ours. In the last chapter of that book I identified some main themes from the teachings and discussed them. So, this gives you a brief background to where we are now. This present book is also based on trusting my ability to communicate with my guides in spirit, and to bring through what they have to say, in this instance to now give us insights about the spirit worlds *per se*. Whilst I do find it remarkably easy to receive their thoughts telepathically, I do not consider myself to be a medium in the usual sense of that term, namely as someone who specifically provides evidence of survival after death. Nor am I a clairvoyant and certainly not an initiate such as Steiner undoubtedly was. I do however regard myself as a 'questioner and researcher', in keeping with my previous university-based projects and enquiries.

The sort of questions I will put to the guides in this book are those which I can imagine you as readers may also be asking yourselves. Thereby I hope we shall be able to gain many useful insights into these non-physical dimensions, enabling a real picture to emerge as to what they are like and what we may expect to find when we pass through the portal of death. Actually it is my conviction that we are *already* in the midst of these spirit worlds during our earthly lives, but lacking the necessary organs of perception for them we remain oblivious of their reality. In a sense we are fast asleep to the spirit in which we now live, just as we are to the sense-world when in ordinary deep sleep. A main aim of inner spiritual development and training, say through meditation, prayer and contemplation, is to awaken our awareness of the invisible worlds in which we are already immersed. It is not a question of going up into 'heaven' in any spatial sense, but rather of learning how to raise our own vibrations and lift our consciousness into those higher dimensions of existence. In several of his key books, Rudolf Steiner described the methods he recommended by which a person can train his or herself to gain an awareness of higher worlds. To be able to actually move consciously within these spiritual domains and to investigate them, it is necessary to learn how to leave our physical body at will and then to remain awake in that body-free state. Of course, we all excarnate quite naturally whenever we fall asleep, but without inner training we do not have the necessary strength of soul to then be fully awake to our spirit surroundings. I also have not acquired such an ability at this stage of my development. However, the aptitude to receive communications from those beings already living in spirit worlds is something quite distinct from going into those regions ourselves. I do believe that many more people could acquire this latter ability, to some degree at least, than those who can become conscious investigators of the higher worlds. Practise, genuine motivation, openness, and good intent is however needed for such inner spirit dialogue.

Each of the following chapters begins then with an overall question, a main theme we could say, to put to the guides. Within that broad theme other questions will no doubt emerge. Even though I cannot enter consciously into spirit worlds myself, I will ask those who *are* living there to tell us something about them through these intentional sessions with my guides. We will then see who, on each occasion, wishes to step forward to answer my enquiries. I am looking forward to seeing where this research process will take us, and will aim to keep an open mind about the contents received. Quite deliberately I have not done any prior reading or study in preparation for working with the guides, since I wish to simply record what they say directly. The various chapter commentaries will therefore only be written sometime after I have received all the communications from the guides.

The guides that I am in contact with are the following:

1. *Joshua Isaiah* – in a former life he was a Jewish Rabbi.
2. *Dr John* – in a former life he was a medical doctor living in the USA.
3. *Markos* – in a former life he was a Greek monk and philosopher.
4. *Red Cloud* – in a former life he was a chief of the Sioux Native Americans.
5. *Raja Lampa* – in a former life he was a Tibetan Lama.
6. *Pierre* – in a former life in France he was a member of the Knights Templar.
7. *Pan* – the Lord of Nature.
8. *Philip* – my guardian angel.

For those who may be wondering if the guides are simply a product of my own imagination, it is important to say that my two clairvoyant friends, Anne Lewis and Neil Castleton, have independently vouched for their reality. Indeed, Neil and I had regular clairvoyant research sessions, designed to consistently identify my guides. These gave good results and all eight guides showed themselves to Neil's clairvoyant perception in various ways.

So, let us now begin this unique enquiry with the first research question, and see where this dialogue will take us when discussing spirit guides *per se*. I would suggest that readers could, if they wish, visualise themselves sat in a circle with the guides in order to enter into these conversations. I would also recommend an alert and receptive attitude, whilst at the same time feeling quite free to ask whatever questions come to mind. In this way you and I will be in tune with each other and the guides. All the conversations which now follow are reproduced verbatim and without any editing on my part.

4
SPIRIT GUIDES

Who are Spirit Guides and How can They Help Us?

Bob: Joshua, I wonder if you and the other guides are willing to speak with me on the theme of 'Who are spirit guides?' What do you think please?

Joshua: Shalom, my friend. Yes, we are more than willing to speak with you on this theme, and we think that it is a good idea to have this also included in the book.

Bob: Right Joshua, do you or someone else wish to start the conversation on this?

Raja: I would like to begin please.

Bob: Raja Lampa, *who* exactly are spirit guides? Can you enlighten me?

Raja: Yes, my friend, I can. Spirit guides are those beings who are there to help human beings on their forward path through life. They are there to assist them in every way that they can, and to be of service and help to them. This is the task of spirit guides.

Bob: Right, but who exactly are spirit guides? I mean, are they human beings now living in spirit, who take up this particular task or role?

Raja: Yes, they are, but not only. There are also other beings – spiritual beings *per se* – who act as spirit guides also.

Bob: Can you elaborate on this please?

Raja: Yes, certainly. So, as well as human beings who live in spirit and who volunteer, shall I say, to take on this particular role, there are also beings from the ranks of the angels, and even archangels and archai, who will act in this capacity. (NB: *There are said to be nine levels or hierarchies of spiritual beings, ranging from the angels and archangels to the cherubim and seraphim.*)

Bob: I'm sorry Raja Lampa, did I understand this aright that you can even include archangels and archai in this role?

Raja: Yes, you did receive this aright. You have asked about *who* are spirit guides, and I am telling you that spirit beings of various ranks, or orders of development, can and do take on these tasks.

Bob: Well Raja Lampa, I am open to that idea, but when I ask who are spirit guides I am really thinking of guides who help and work with individual people on Earth – like myself for example. I don't imagine that the higher spirits you refer to are engaged just with individuals, but maybe whole groups of people? Am I right in this?

Raja: Yes you are quite right in this. I have been describing those who are working as spirit guides in the widest possible context, which includes peoples, nations and the whole of humanity. In that sense there are hierarchical beings who try to guide and help the whole of humanity towards reaching their goal.

Bob: Right, Raja Lampa. Could we then for this chapter just restrict ourselves to guides who work with individuals please, because I think this is of the greatest relevance to our readers?

Raja: Yes, we can do that. What do you want to know about them?

Bob: Well, what determines if a human being after death, living in spirit, will become a spirit guide to someone in the body?

Raja: Well this depends on their own wishes and inclinations. If this is the way that they choose to serve others, then this is the task or role which they can take up.

Bob: But does this then need some training to do this effectively or can someone just jump into doing this?

Raja: Yes it requires guidance from those who have greater experience in these matters. So yes, a person cannot simply 'jump into' the role as you put it, but they need to be guided themselves by those who have knowledge and experience.

Bob: Right, Raja Lampa. I am trying to imagine more concrete examples of all this, so that people really get a clear idea of what is happening. So let me ask, can departed family members, for example, become guides to those of their family still on Earth? For example, could my own mother and father now in spirit become guides to me?

Raja: Yes, they could indeed if that was their wish to do so. Yes, many family members who have attained the necessary degree of clarity and awareness in spirit could be offered to take on such roles for their family left on Earth.

Bob: So are you saying, Raja Lampa, that spirit guides are often departed family members? Is that what you mean?

Raja: Yes that is what I mean, but this should not be seen in too narrow a sense. Remember you have lived on Earth many times and so your 'family', so to speak, includes many, many people – not just the family from your present lifetime. So it is good to see what I'm saying in this extended time-frame, and not just confined to the more immediate scenario.

Bob: Right, I can see this. So again as an example, in my case would the spirit guides that I am now aware of have been part of my extended family, so to speak, covering perhaps many previous lifetimes or incarnations?

Raja: Yes indeed, that is exactly what I mean my friend. I also am related to you through your previous incarnations in Tibet, when you were a monk living in Lhasa. So here, you see, we have our link and in similar ways you have links with the other guides that you know of so far.

Bob: Well Raja I can accept, or at least imagine this, but obviously this wouldn't apply to my links with Pan and with Philip, correct?

Raja: Yes, that is correct of course since they are on a different evolutionary pathway. However we are confining ourselves now to the human links – the links between human beings who are all on the same evolutionary journey.

Bob: Raja, do you think that there are other guides who would also like to contribute to this theme?

Raja: Yes there are, and I am happy to step back so that someone else can now step forward.

Red Cloud: I would like to continue here.

Bob: Thank you, Red Cloud. Can I ask this – is there differentiation re. spirit guides who help a particular person on Earth? I mean, would a person have a *main* guide say, whereas the other guides then have a lesser role to play, or how is this?

Red Cloud: Well my friend, you could compare it to living in a tribe such as I did when I lived as a Native American, hundreds of years ago. I mean that within a tribe there are different roles to fulfil for the sake of the whole tribe. Not everyone performs the same functions. Some people are better at hunting, shall we say, others better at homemaking, others better at looking after the herds of bison or whatever, others better at tracking, others at building tepees, etc. etc. Different roles within the whole, you get my drift? So similarly, in the work of guides, there are different sorts of tasks to take on. So you may have one guide for this and another guide for that particular task. You know already about so-called spirit doctors, you know that they have their particular healing tasks – that they guide and help those involved in healing work on Earth. This is their role.

However, others can be involved in teaching or education you could say, others in helping with particular professions or vocations. Let's say for example that someone is a scientist engaged in good work for others, a needed role on Earth. Then this scientist can be helped by someone in spirit who is familiar with their area of work, their expertise you could say. So you see, you can imagine that in all manner of ways, help and guidance can be offered from spirit to those who are working on Earth.

Bob: Well yes, I can imagine this also. But what about mundane but very necessary earthly tasks or jobs? Say a plumber, electrician, builder, etc., would such people have specialist guides in these areas?

Red Cloud: Well not quite. We don't have plumbers and electricians in spirit, but we do have people, spirit people, who will know what sort of help and support is needed by those on Earth who are living those sort of lives. After all, even though someone may be a plumber on Earth, he or she is still a human being who has much to cope with in life, not just pipes and fittings, but also a family, finance, friends and relations, etc. So guidance can be given to help a person with all these problems, or rather challenges.

Bob: So, Red Cloud, I think what you're saying is that, perhaps, each person, each individual, can have or is assigned spirit guides to help them in the ways they most need?

Red Cloud: Yes that is a very good way of putting it. Depending on that person's position in life, their mindset, their views, their needs, so suitable guides can be given to support and help them.

Bob: So are our guides 'hand-picked', as it were, for each individual, each person?

Red Cloud: Yes, they are. Each person attracts towards him or herself the guides in spirit whom he or she needs at any time. So you, my friend, have attracted me and other guides to work with you on your books, and we are happy to assist you with them.

Bob: Does every person, every human being, have his or her spirit guides, or only some people?

Red Cloud: Every person has at least one spirit guide, and some people have more than one guide assisting them at any one time.

Bob: So if people were conscious of this then they would discover, shall I say, that they are being helped, supported, by their guides day by day. Is that right?

Red Cloud: Yes, that is right. There is an ongoing working going on between individuals and their guides, though mostly this takes place unconsciously.

Bob: Red Cloud, you realise that many people may laugh at this idea that they have guides helping them?

Red Cloud: Yes, they may indeed, but this doesn't change the facts of the matter.

Bob: But Red Cloud, surely guides cannot infringe on a person's free will and choice, can they?

Red Cloud: No they cannot, but still they are there to help in every way that they can.

Bob: Can they help if a person is totally unaware of them?

Red Cloud: Yes, they can actually, because a person is only totally unaware in their normal day-to-day consciousness, but not so in their higher consciousness.

Bob: Right Red Cloud, thank you. I think that here I'll stop for now. Is that alright?

Red Cloud: Yes, it is perfectly alright. All blessings, Red Cloud.

Bob: Joshua, I have to ask you please, have I really been receiving the communications correctly this morning or not?

Joshua: Shalom, my friend. Yes you have. Please trust in your own abilities to do this. All blessings, Joshua Isaiah.

*[1]

Bob: Joshua, I would like to continue with the theme of 'Who are spirit guides?' Is that alright?

Joshua: Shalom, my friend. Yes, it is perfectly alright. We are there to assist you when you link up with us for that purpose.

Bob: Well Joshua, let me ask this. I think of you as my *main* spirit guide, if I can put it like that. So, do you see yourself in that capacity also?

Joshua: Shalom, my friend. Yes, I do, since you have me as your first point of contact, so to speak, unless of course you ask John for something to do with your healing work. So yes, in that sense, I am your main spirit guide.

Bob: Are spirit guides sometimes referred to as 'gatekeepers', and if so, who is that for each person?

Joshua: Yes, my friend, this is a term which has been used to describe us and it simply means that we then have the role of providing safe entry and passage into spirit worlds for you.

Bob: What does that mean then, since I don't go into spirit worlds, do I?

Joshua: Yes you do, all the time, but you are often not conscious of it. I am then the gatekeeper for you, and see that you are protected and helped to enter safely.

Bob: Now Joshua, I am quite confused because I thought, I believe, what you're describing here is really the role of the so-called 'guardian of the threshold' – that's what Rudolf Steiner refers to, at least.

Joshua: Yes, this is correct. There is the guardian of the threshold that you refer to, but there is also the role which I as your main guide perform

[1] An asterisk in the text indicates the end of a session.

for you. It is in many ways a similar sort of role, but is something that I can do easily because we have the link established between us.

Bob: Right, Joshua, well this is a new concept for me and I'll have to think on this some more, particularly as I am not aware of entering spirit worlds *per se*.

Joshua: Yes, we know you think you don't enter them, but in reality you do, and when you do so, I act as the gatekeeper for you.

Bob: Right, Joshua, perhaps I need to find questions which others can relate to. So let me ask, 'How would someone become aware of their own spirit guides?'

Red Cloud: My friend, let me speak here. A person can become aware of their own guide by asking for that guide to make themselves known to him or her. If that request is made, then the guide will find a way of responding to it which is appropriate for that person. In your case it was via the medium, Anne Lewis; with someone else there will be other links which can be used to make the connection.

Bob: Would these links be, for example, with a deceased family member perhaps?

Red Cloud: Yes, it could be like that when the person on Earth is open to that sort of contact. But it could also be by other means, that the person has the feeling or impression that their guide is close to them and willing to help them.

Bob: Can you give examples of that please?

Red Cloud: Yes, I can. Suppose for example that a person is wrestling with a problem or a dilemma which they seem unable to solve for themselves. Suddenly, an idea may occur to them, a sudden thought or inspiration, and this enables them to see a way forward. In this instance their guide has managed to give them the help which they require.

Bob: Right. Another example, please.

Red Cloud: Right, let's say that you are going through a testing time and do not know where to turn to. Suddenly someone turns up and can give you the advice you need. In this case your guide will have guided or led the person towards you, to provide the support you need.

Bob: Red Cloud, I realise that I've strayed off the theme of this chapter, i.e. 'Who are Spirit Guides?' I think I might need to put the main theme differently in order to allow for information which readers will want to read. What do you think?

Red Cloud: That's probably a very good idea, otherwise it can be too restrictive – just broaden your theme to cover other aspects.

NB: I then included, 'How Can They Help Us?' in the overall theme.

Bob: Right Red Cloud. I've just changed it, or rather broadened it, so how *can* spirit guides help us?

Red Cloud: They can help in all manner of ways but, principally, their aim is to give the support needed to the particular individual, the person to whom they have been assigned.

Bob: Isn't this then 'treading on the toes' of the guardian angel?

Red Cloud: Not really, because the guardian angel has quite enough to do in trying to keep the person on track with their own aims and goals in that lifetime. The angel oversees the destiny of the person in their care. However, the guides have a more down-to-earth task, you might say, on a daily basis, of guiding and helping and supporting that person.

Bob: But Red Cloud, what you just described is very much how I imagine the angel also working with their charges.

Red Cloud: Well yes, it is and it isn't. As I said, the angel has a greater overview of what the person in their higher self is striving to achieve, whereas we as guides are more concerned with the day-to-day challenges the person faces.

Bob: So are a person's guides also aware of that person's guardian angel?

Red Cloud: Yes, they are, to an extent. It depends rather on the nature and calibre of the guides as to how aware they are of the angel working with that person. Some are much more attuned to the angelic consciousness level than others.

Bob: Red Cloud, Rudolf Steiner pointed to the importance of cooperation between the living and the dead. He meant of course between those living in the body and those living in spirit. He said, I believe, that the dead would and should become the counsellors of the living. Does this make sense to you?

Red Cloud: Yes, perfect sense. Really, he is here describing the work of spirit guides even though he didn't use that terminology.

Bob: That's interesting, because many followers of Steiner wouldn't think (I think) in those terms at all.

Red Cloud: No, they may not, but nonetheless this is what Rudolf Steiner was pointing to, cooperation between us on both sides of the veil.

Bob: Yes, I can see that. Some people however may have no sense, no idea and no inclination to strike up a contact with friends or guides in spirit. Perhaps they find this too bizarre, or are even scared of this prospect. What do you think?

Red Cloud: Yes, I think you are right in this. Many people would find this idea too strange to consider, particularly as they rarely give any thought to spiritual subjects.

Bob: And is that a pity?

Red Cloud: It certainly is because they miss out on a lot of help and support which they could otherwise receive.

Bob: But don't their guides help them anyway?

Red Cloud: They try to, but you can take a horse to water but you can't make it drink!

Bob: I think fear would play into this as well.

Red Cloud: Yes it does. The whole notion of spirits around will make some people extremely nervous and frightened.

Bob: Which is understandable, isn't it?

Red Cloud: Yes, it is, but only because they have a distorted notion of what spirits are and what they can do.

Bob: Well, this is partly the reason for this book isn't it, to give reassurance and alleviate fear and ignorance?

Red Cloud: Yes, it is, and that is why we are happy to help you in the writing of it.

Bob: Thank you, Red Cloud, I'll stop for now.

Red Cloud: Good, until next time. All blessings, Red Cloud.

*

Bob: Joshua, can I ask further questions re. spirit guides?

Joshua: Shalom, my friend. Yes, fire away.

Bob: Well Joshua, does a person keep the same guide through his or her lifetime, or do the guides change?

Pierre: I would like to answer this. Normally a person will have one main guide who is faithful to them for a long time. This enables a good relationship to be built up between the guide and the person concerned. However, other guides can come and go, depending on that person's particular needs and stages of life. Therefore in answer to your question, it is a variable feast but, usually, one guide is constant and is the main guide or gatekeeper for that individual.

Bob: So Pierre, let's say in my case I consider Joshua as my main guide for teaching, advice and counselling, with John as my main healing guide. Would then other guides I've met, such as yourself, be more temporary and transient to me?

Pierre: Yes and no. In your case, my friend, it is somewhat different because of the work you are doing together with us. You have a much more conscious relationship with us than is the case with most people. Therefore we will be there for you whilst you are engaged in such work and need our help.

Bob: So whilst my book-writing and research continues I can count on you, Pierre, and the others?

Pierre: Yes you can. We are there to assist you in every way that we can.

Bob: Thank you all. What about the situation as I presume it is for many people, that they go through life totally oblivious to the fact that they have spirit guides ready to help them?

Pierre: Well, in these cases, which are many, all the guides can do is to be patient and wait until the right moment comes for the person to wake up. This may be through a shock of some kind, perhaps bereavement, or some other crisis in their lives when they desperately need support.

Bob: But how then can guides make their presence felt or known?

Pierre: Well, in the sorts of ways touched upon already. By giving the person a particular feeling or thought or sense of being watched over and helped in some way they do not fully understand. Basically, guides will do whatever it takes to help people wake up to their reality – their real presence – save encroaching on anyone's free will.

Bob: Do guides ever force themselves, so to speak, on to people?

Pierre: Definitely not, if their motivations and intentions are good.

Bob: But could there be some guides who would seek to interfere or influence people unjustly, shall we say?

Pierre: If there are any guides who would do that, then they are not true guides. The guides will never encroach upon a person's free will, decisions or choices.

Bob: Thank you Pierre, I will have to stop now. Many thanks.

Pierre: You are very welcome.

*

Bob: Joshua, do guides, even main guides like yourself, work with more than one person during a period of time?

Joshua: Shalom, my friend. Yes, we do work with a number of people. Our work is not restricted to just one person on Earth because we are able to be helpful to others also. So yes, although I am your main guide, so to speak, I do also work with other individuals who are needing the help which I can give.

Bob: Well Joshua, that might mean, I suppose – say in my case – that a person feels less special – that they don't have that guide just to themselves alone?

Joshua: Yes, that could be the case. But on the other hand, a person could also feel grateful that their guide is able to assist and help other people also. After all, it is not good to adopt a selfish attitude towards one's relationship with one's guides, is it?

Bob: Well, I can see that. The only thing is, though, that a person might feel that the guide does not give them their undivided attention!

Joshua: Well, that is actually not so. When I work with you, Bob, you do have my undivided attention, but when I work with someone else, they also have my undivided attention at that time.

Bob: But Joshua, how is that really possible because, as you know, I can call upon you, speak with you at any time. We do not have fixed appointments for our conversations.

Joshua: Yes, you are right in this, my friend. I can respond to you whenever you ask, but bear in mind that my consciousness is not limited or restricted in the same way it is when living in a dense physical body. So I can easily multi-task and be with yourself and someone else, if need be, simultaneously.

Bob: Well Joshua, that's a difficult idea for me to take on board.

Joshua: Yes, we know this can be difficult for you to imagine, but nonetheless, what I have told you is true.

Bob: Well Joshua, that's certainly very interesting and new to me.

Joshua: Yes, it is new to you, but please take it on board as something new which you have learnt today. All blessings, Joshua Isaiah.

Bob: Thank you. I will.

*

Bob: Joshua, if I think of you as a teacher in spirit, which is the case, then of course a teacher can have numerous pupils. In earthly terms, a teacher can have a class of pupils that he or she is responsible for guiding and helping. Not so?

Joshua: Shalom, my friend. Precisely so. Yes that is a good point you raise and this enables you to understand that my work is not only with you but includes others also. Yes, a good analogy to use for my role and function. Thank you.

Bob: And actually, Joshua, I suppose, or can imagine, that this is similar for John as a spirit doctor. That he probably works with other healers and not just myself?

Joshua: Precisely, my friend. Yes, John is connected with other healers on Earth, and together with his team can work through them to benefit their patients and clients. Yes, this again is a good thought to understand how we work from spirit.

Commentary

What my guides have described here about the nature of spirit guides and their various roles with us are ,I would say, validated by Ruth White (1971 & 2004) and James Van Praagh (2017) in their respective books. Both of these authors are widely acknowledged as having many years of experience in working with their own guides.

Ruth White's main guide is known by the name of 'Gildas' and when answering queries about making the link with one's own guide he said that,

> The way to contact is open to all; the rewards are great. It cannot be too highly recommended as the inner way which each should eventually strive to follow. Pray for the conscious knowledge of your guide, be receptive, trust hunches, ask for help when a decision has to be made and learn to follow the voice of your guide.

He then adds,

> Prayer and meditation are the main ways to achieving contact, since the way must be opened in quietness for an inner communion with your guides. (White & Swainson 1971, p.144)

In Ruth's much more recent publication entitled, *Working with Spirit Guides*, she says the following,

> Spirit guides are evolved beings. They will have some close spiritual or soul level link to us, but being a guide is their 'job'. They are helping us and watching over us, whether we make a conscious effort to connect with them or not. Once we connect with them through conscious and specific effort and training we will come to know them as our best friends and wise advisers.

Moreover,

> Relatives apart, almost certainly we will have known our spirit guides before. We will have met them in some other incarnation, and perhaps in several other incarnations.

Interestingly, she also notes that,

> We certainly can, and probably most of us do, have more than one spirit guide. (White 2004, pp.29-31)

In his recent book, *Wisdom from your Spirit Guides*, James Van Praagh writes,

> Welcome to the vast and expansive world of guides! Our guides occupy an infinite array of spiritual dimensions and may have never incarnated at all, or they can be family members

> and friends who we have known in this lifetime, and who have since made the transition to spirit. Whoever they may be, guides have a keen interest in your development as a soul, and they work with you as personal teachers to inspire, influence, motivate, protect, and direct you throughout your lifetime.
>
> Many of your guides have been with you in a variety of lifetimes; some show up for one lifetime, or for a portion of your life, or even perhaps just a fleeting moment. Guides are our friends, helping us to fulfil our destiny. Some are with us merely to comfort and encourage us when things are difficult and unsettling.

Importantly, he also maintains that,

> Everyone can connect with their guides. Soul-to-soul connections happen all the time, but most people don't recognise them as such. For instance, whenever you think of a deceased loved one, you probably assume the thought began with you. More probable is that your loved one (with the help of your guide) is sending the thought to you. (Van Praagh 2017, pp.3-4)

In Steiner's anthroposophy the notion of guidance from spiritual beings, both for humanity as a whole and for the individual, is also a central theme. For example, in his book written in 1911, *The Spiritual Guidance of Man and Humanity*, Steiner speaks, in evolutionary terms, of the wise guidance given us from the angels but also points out that,

> Above these beings in ascending order, stand those of the higher hierarchies, the archangels, the archai, and so forth, who likewise take part in the guidance of humanity. (Steiner 1983, p.51)

However, in respect of the working of the angels *per se*, in this same book he says that,

> We are now approaching the time when people are to become conscious of these guiding powers.(p.78)

This indicates a new step or development in our spiritual awareness as human beings. Whilst Steiner may not have spoken of 'spirit guides', as this term is now used by myself and other contemporary authors, he certainly did speak of the helpful influence of our relatives and friends who have gone through the portal of death and now live in spirit worlds. He significantly pointed out that the so-called dead can become 'counsellors' for the living and even stated that,

> All historical life – all social life, all ethical life – proceeds by virtue of cooperation between the so-called living and the so-called dead. (Steiner 1999b, p.161)

Clearly Steiner, already in the early part of the twentieth century, anticipated that a much more conscious and cooperative way of working between ourselves and our friends in spirit should come about in future. To my mind, this cooperation is synonymous with linking-in with our own spirit guides, which can certainly include our personal guardian angels (see Steiner, 2000). In another recent book we find the following comment when referring to those who have already passed through death.

> Those who are sufficiently mature and who have achieved a certain degree of wisdom and love can often serve as a guide for loved ones who have remained on earth. We not only have our own guardian angels who help us and support us on our path through this life, we also may have one or more guides, loved ones who have died who can guide us through earthly life and the spiritual world. Many people are intuitively aware of such loving guidance. (Brink & Stolp 2017, p.45)

Interestingly, James Van Praagh (2017) refers to the term 'gatekeeper' as a person's spirit guide who is responsible for guarding the portal between the spiritual and physical worlds. He also makes a distinction between a person's 'master guide', or main guide, and their gatekeeper. However, it seems that Joshua assumes both roles in my case, and is both teacher and protector.

Whilst I would recommend that interested readers can turn to the additional literature I have referred to here, the important point is that the existence of spirit guides is amply confirmed by these other sources. Moreover, my own conscious and cooperative work with my guides, from its first beginnings fifteen years ago and right up to the present time, is explicitly described in the books, *Spirit Communications* (2007), *Trusting in Spirit, The Challenge* (2018) and this current volume. Taken together, they really do form something of a unique spiritual trilogy. My hope is that they will encourage others to gain awareness of their own guides.

References

Brink, M van den & Stolp, H. (2017) *What Happens When We Die? Our Journey in the Afterlife.* Temple Lodge

Steiner, R. (1983) *The Spiritual Guidance of Man and Humanity.* Anthroposophic Press

Steiner, R. (1999b) *Staying Connected – How to continue your relationships with those who have died.* Anthroposophic Press

Steiner, R. (2000) *Guardian Angels – Connecting with our Spiritual Guides and Helpers.* Rudolf Steiner Press

Van Praagh, J. (2017) *Wisdom from your Spirit Guides.* Hay House

White, R. & Swainson, M. (1971) *Gildas Communicates.* Neville Spearman

White, R. (2004) *Working with Spirit Guides.* Piatkus

5
AFTER DEATH

What Happens After We Die?

Bob: Joshua, I would like if possible to make a start on the theme of this chapter, namely 'What happens after we die?' This theme certainly concerns us all, since our earthly death is an inevitability. Therefore, whatever happens after our death is, to say the least, certainly of real interest. Are you and the other guides willing to answer this question for us?

Joshua: Shalom, my friend, yes, we are. As you say, it is a question which concerns everyone, even those who are out and out materialists – even they cannot escape the inevitability of death.

Bob: Right Joshua, who wants to begin this?

Philip: I would like to start this theme off. Yes, I am an angel, not a human being, but still I am very much engaged in helping the process of death – that is the process of re-birth into spirit – to go well. I have done this many times before for you, my friend! So your question is, 'What happens after we die?'

In the first place of course we need to point out that you don't die. Only your physical, material, body dies. That is to say, your material body goes back to where it came from, to the substances of Mother Earth. You yourself, however, live on. You immediately feel the lightness of being when you are removed from the heaviness of your earthly sheath. You feel liberated, provided of course that you can overcome your initial fears. Yes, fear of death, fear of dying, can hold a person back from experiencing the joy of liberation from the body. This joy is, however, there for the person, the human being, who puts his or her trust in the powers that be. That is, the powers, the beings, that oversee the physical death process. These are angel beings and also other higher spirits who safeguard the process for the human being. You are never left alone, you are never abandoned; always spirits watch over you to help you make the great transition.

We realise that from the human point of view the transition or passing into spirit is a momentous event. True, you – I mean most human beings – have gone through this same event many times in the past, but still you have no clear memory of those occasions. So when you come to it again, it is like a completely new experience. However my friends, let me reassure you all that this event is guarded over and protected by spirits who are dedicated to help you. So this is the first thing that needs to be said about what happens when you die.

Bob: Thank you Philip, this certainly sounds most reassuring to me. What does the person who has just died experience, what are they aware of?

Joshua: My friend, let me jump in here, so to speak. Well, you know that you have read descriptions which tell that the person sees a big picture, a complete picture as it were, of their past life, and this is true. When you die, my friend, your whole life is revealed to you in one great vision. Now, that is quite something to behold! You really do see everything you have ever done. Of course you may now be thinking, my friend, that surely that is not possible. How can you possibly see everything you have ever done, even into the details, the minutiae of life?

Well, however difficult this may be for you to grasp, nonetheless it is true. You look on your life as if it is spread out before you on a large painting canvas. You yourself are the artist. It is your picture, your very own creation. So, whether it altogether pleases you or not, whether you think that you really need to paint this part anew or at least touch-up, nonetheless there it stands before you to begin with. This picture will be there for you for a few of your earth days only. Your angel also has the memory of this. It is another page in your book of life. After that experience, your journey into the spirit worlds really begins and you start to walk forwards, shall we say.

Bob: Joshua, can I just clarify something about the whole life-picture that appears to a person after their death? When I telepathically spoke to my friend who died a few days ago, he said the life-picture was like a sphere around him; that living pictures of his life were around him on all sides and he experienced himself looking at them as from the centre of that sphere. Is this a true description – did I receive this correctly from him?

Joshua: Shalom, my friend, yes you did. Yes, it is a very good description of how this is actually experienced after death. The life-picture completely surrounds the person, rather than being on a flat screen say as in a cinema. No, it is rather a living being, an entity in itself that surrounds the person beholding it. It is there in all details, colour, animation – a truly living thing that is beheld.

Bob: So is it really, you could say, like the universe, the world, in which a person is placed at the centre looking out at it?

Joshua: Yes, that is a good way of putting it. The person is at the centre of his life-world, witnessing all that he or she has ever done in the life that has just passed. It is a wonderful opportunity to see everything displayed before him or her.

Bob: How long is this experience?

Joshua: Only as long as the 'ether body', as you call it, remains in connection with the physical body and is held together by the physical link, so to speak. When that link ceases, then the ether body dissolves and the life-picture fades away.

Bob: So about three days?

Joshua: Yes, about three days, though it can vary a little. It is not absolutely fixed.

Bob: Thank you, Joshua.

Bob: Well, Joshua, the life-picture you have described I have certainly read about before, but what happens next, and are we alone? Do we not meet our family and friends that have gone before us?

Joshua: Yes, you certainly do. This belongs to the journey, the adventure you might say, that you now undertake. Yes, you will meet all those with whom you are connected through love and affection. They will come to greet you and welcome you into your new life. They will have been waiting for this moment and they will have known as soon as you crossed the threshold from your earthly life to this one.

Bob: Is all this a joyful event, I mean this reunion with our family and friends?

Joshua: Yes, it is indeed. It is a time of great happiness, you could say. You know for certain that they have been waiting to see you on their side of life. On this side of 'the river', you could say. Now you have reached their shores. Well done my friend!

Bob: Joshua, how long does this reunion last?

Joshua: It lasts a long time, but we can really not speak of time as you do on Earth. On Earth your lives are ruled by time, but in spirit it is different. Yes, there are events which come and go, but their going just means that they are further behind you but still visible in the distance. The events in which you take place now are immediate and take up all your attention. You live much more strongly, shall I say, than you did, usually, on Earth. Your mind is sharper because you are not distracted by the body *per se*. Everything becomes easier for you, because you are lighter and freer in yourself. It is a new way of being *you*.

Bob: Joshua, thank you. I would like to stop there for now and resume this theme tomorrow morning; is that alright?

Joshua: Yes, perfectly alright. We will work with you whenever you are ready, but it is up to you to tell us when. All blessings, Joshua Isaiah.

Bob: Thank you again.

*

Bob: Joshua, I am keen to continue our conversation of yesterday evening on the theme of, 'What happens after we die?' because I feel this is of great interest to many of us. After all, we are all heading in that direction – I mean all of us who are at present alive on the Earth. Are you and the other guides willing to work with me on this now?

Joshua: Shalom, my friend. Yes, we certainly are. May I suggest you see who would like to come through first for you?

Bob: Yes, thank you. But first can I say that I am interested to pick up on where we left off yesterday. After the big picture of our lives and being greeted by our friends in spirit, then I think we start on our journey into spirit. Was that it?

Markos: I would like to start with this, my friend. Yes, the journey into spirit, the walking as it were into those dimensions of experience and reality where you gain truer knowledge of who you are, because this is really what this journey is about. You are getting closer, journeying you could say, towards the essential essence of your being. In order to do that, you need to go through those experiences which will help you to see clearly what lies at the centre of your being.

Bob: Markos, I want to know more about this but I am also aware that my previous reading about this subject, mainly in Steiner's work, may colour whatever you say. On the other hand, I do wish to be as open as I can to just bring through what you and the other guides relate to me.

Markos: Don't worry about this, my friend, simply note down, write, what you receive from us. Later you may wish to draw comparisons between what you have read before and what we give to you, but for now simply bring through what we give you, please.

Bob: Right, that's what I will do.

Markos: Good. Now, about this journey, this way into the spirit worlds. You need, and when I say you, I mean this applying to all human beings who have died, you need to experience again what you did in your last life on Earth; to experience it now from a different point of view, a different level of existence. Before, you were immersed in your earthly body and in your day-to-day existence. Now you are freed from all that and you have the possibility to view things, and experience things, from a quite different angle. You can now experience how you have affected others throughout your life.

It is no longer your pointwise experience, your personal experience of what you did, said or thought, but now you see it all through the eyes of others, so to speak. You experience what they went through because of what you did, said or thought. 'The shoe is on the other foot,' and you will experience both the joys and sorrows, the ups and downs, the blows of fate, the achievements and triumphs, all from their side of life. Not from your personal experience as Tom Smith or Mr Jones, or whoever you happened to be in life.

Bob: Markos, this that you describe is very much what I have previously understood to be the case.

Markos: Yes, your previous readings have given you a true picture of the process to be gone through on this initial journeying into spirit, that is, towards the essence of who you really are.

Bob: Markos, I'll take a break please.

Markos: Yes, by all means do so, we can resume when you are ready.

*

Bob: Joshua, I've had a short break, can we now continue please?

Joshua: Shalom, my friend, of course we can. Let us see who wishes to come through next to enlighten you.

Pierre: I would like to step in now please.

Bob: Right Pierre, can you tell me more about what Markos was describing?

Pierre: Yes, my friend, I can. Now, as regards the journey after death, it is really a journey of self-discovery. This is really what it is about, a learning to see who you were in your earthly life, not now from your limited personal viewpoint, but from the impact which your life had on others. After all, you were often quite unaware of what effect you were having on those whom you met, perhaps briefly, or those whom you lived with for a longer time, perhaps for years. So this is what is necessary, a re-examining of your own life from a higher perspective.

Bob: Pierre, yes this makes perfect sense to me, but how long does all this last? I have read that we can spend about one third of our earthly lifetime going through this examining process. Is that right?

Pierre: Well, yes it is and it isn't. It depends very much on the person. Some people will need that length of time, so to speak, others won't.

Bob: So what does it depend on?

Pierre: It depends on what work they have done previously to get to know themselves from outside, so to speak.

Bob: From 'outside' – what does that mean?

Pierre: It means to be able to look at themselves with some objectivity, instead of taking everything very personally.

Bob: Is that where inner training, say through meditation and other exercises, makes a difference?

Pierre: Precisely so. The person who has made efforts in life to come to terms with themselves, to reassess themselves and their actions, feelings, etc., is in a better position to move on more quickly after death.

Bob: Right, but to move on to what? What comes next?

Pierre: Well, after the period of time spent in reassessing and re-experiencing your last life you are then ready to make a further ascent, we can say, into higher dimensions of reality.

Bob: To do what?

Pierre: To start to make plans about what direction you want to go in, about what you want to do.

Bob: This sounds a bit strange to me. Sounds more like planning for a career move!

Pierre: Yes it does my friend, but remember I am having to use language that is comprehensible to you. I need to express myself so that you can form a clear picture of what I am talking about.

Bob: Yes, I can see that, otherwise of course I shall have no idea.

Pierre: Yes, so that is why it comes across as it does.

Bob: Is it then that we are passing through, or journeying, into different regions or dimensions of spirit worlds after we die. Is that what is happening?

Pierre: Yes, this is a good way of putting it. You travel into different regions, places, of the spirit world in order to progress, stage by stage, towards finding yourself.

Bob: Do you mean to say that after death I won't immediately find my true, spirit, self?

Pierre: Yes, that's what I am saying my friend. It is a process, a journeying, towards that goal and you need to be guided along that route so that you can safely come to yourself.

Bob: Pierre, I am wondering if I need to turn soon then to the next chapter and main theme, which will be, 'Where do we live?' What do you think?

Pierre: I think that is probably a very good idea and that to do this will help you to picture more clearly what it is like where we live as your spirit guides.

Bob: In that case, Pierre, thank you and I will bring this session to a close. Joshua, I hope I am bringing through correctly what the other guides are telling me?

Joshua: Shalom, my friend, fear not, you are well able to communicate with us and to bring it through correctly. Well done, my friend. All blessings, Joshua Isaiah.

Bob: Thank you, Joshua.

NB: Now I actually decided to take as the main theme for the next chapter, 'Spirit Worlds' rather than 'Where do we live?' which we will turn to in Chapter 7. However, I also wanted to ask some further questions which still belong to this chapter.

*

Bob: Joshua, can you say more about what happens to us after we have re-experienced our life from the viewpoint of others? That is after we have experienced the impact, the effects, we have had on them. What happens next to us? For example, do we take up specific tasks or roles in the higher dimensions?

Joshua: Shalom, my friend. In answer to your question let me say the following. After you have learnt, from the experiences of others, of your own past life, then you are ready to move on in the spirit worlds. With the knowledge and insights which you have acquired through your life's assessment, you are in a much better position to become clear about what needs to be done. For example, how to balance out your karmic debts and to follow through with your responsibilities. You realise much more clearly than before, that the progress of the world and of mankind depends upon each person, each soul, taking responsibility for their own actions. You realise that in order to bring about a balance in your life and the lives of others, you must see that you compensate for any errors on your part which have caused distress and unhappiness to others. So this, my friend, very much determines how you will get on, and move on, within the spirit worlds.

Bob: Okay Joshua, I accept that each person will need to feel responsible for their actions and, shall we say, put things right that may, or have, gone wrong. So how do we go about this in terms of our onward journey into higher dimensions?

Joshua: You go about this, my friend, by coming to certain clarities about what is needed. You see, with others who can help and guide you, how best to make amends for your errors or omissions, or actual bad deeds, if you committed any.

Bob: So are you saying, Joshua, that the journey into spirit involves us working out, or planning, how to do things better next time on Earth, if we reincarnate? Or can we just sort it out in the spirit worlds?

Joshua: No, you can't just sort it all out in spirit. In spirit you can form your clear intentions and see clearly what needs to be done, but the actual doing needs to take place on the same plane of action where your karma has accrued.

Bob: So are you saying, Joshua, that during our time in spirit we are already planning for our next earthly life?

Joshua: Yes, exactly. It is necessary to formulate your plan of action and this is helped by the spirits, the beings, who are assigned to assist you in this.

Bob: Well Joshua, if it is a matter of sorting out, or balancing, our karma with those that we knew or met in our last earth-life, then will those souls also need to reincarnate with us? A sort of group-destiny, you might say.

Joshua: Yes, that is right. You will meet the same souls that you encountered in your last life, but the relationships you have with them in the next life will almost certainly be different and give new opportunities for growth and learning.

Bob: Joshua, I can see this, however, coming back still to the onward journey after we have died, do we take up specific tasks, jobs, roles, in spirit, or not?

Joshua: Yes, you can do. There are certain possibilities which will also enable you to serve the needs of others by the roles and tasks which you take up.

Bob: Right, Joshua. Actually one of the following chapters has to do with, 'What do we do in spirit?', so perhaps further questions on this theme should wait for that chapter?

Joshua: Yes, that would be a good plan.

Bob: Thank you, Joshua. I still have another question though. I think Rudolf Steiner talked about travelling through the different planetary spheres after death, and eventually arriving at the starry cosmos *per se*. Is this right; can you understand this?

Red Cloud: I would like to answer this one. Yes, your teacher Rudolf Steiner was quite right in describing the journey after death in this way.

There are these different planes, spheres, regions – call them what you will. The important point is that they are qualitatively different and distinct, and that as you pass through them or some of them, you can have very different sorts of experiences.

Bob: Do you mean, for example, that if I go through the Mars-sphere, say, this will be a different experience than passing through the Venus plane, and so on?

Red Cloud: Yes, that is exactly what I mean. You will feel attracted to this or that plane or region, more or less depending on your disposition, make-up, beliefs, upbringing, etc. So there are some planes where you will go through them quickly, because they do not attract you especially, but there will be others where you find much in common with those beings who live there.

Bob: What's the point of all this then?

Red Cloud: The point is that you are getting to know yourself on deeper and deeper levels of being. You are finding your true identity, through the experiences you are having after your earthly death.

Bob: So will I, will we, eventually come in our journey to really know ourselves as spirit beings?

Red Cloud: Yes you will, and when you do, your whole world of experience is very different from what you have known before. The cloaks which concealed you from yourself are thrown off, and you stand in full vision of your God-like Self.

Bob: Wouldn't this fuel our egotism and narcissism?

Red Cloud: No it doesn't, because all that belongs to the 'lower you' which has been left behind you.

Bob: So is this, then, the ultimate goal of our journey in the afterlife – to realise who we really are?

Red Cloud: Yes, it is, because only then can you see clearly how you can contribute to the good of the world, to the cosmos, through your knowledge and goodwill.

Bob: Well that sounds good, but it is difficult for me to see where we get to next after this.

Red Cloud: After this you are ready to begin your descent towards the Earth again, and see what you can accomplish to help the world move forward.

Bob: So is this, then, God's plan, we could say, for the human race as a whole?

Red Cloud: Yes, it is. It is a glorious plan for evolution and transformation, which needs human beings to become awake to their spiritual selfhood.

Bob: Right Red Cloud, I think that's as far as I can go for now, thank you.

Red Cloud: Thank you, my friend, for what you are doing. All blessings, Red Cloud.

*

Bob: Joshua, I still actually have one more question on this theme, namely what sort of consciousness do we have after death, to begin with and then later on? On Earth we have our point-centred self-consciousness. Does this continue after death also?

Joshua: Shalom, my friend. Yes, we can answer this question for you. After death your consciousness is expanded. You no longer have the restricted, point-centred consciousness that is your normal day-awake awareness. Instead you grow beyond yourselves. Your mind expands enormously and you feel that you are a part of the wider cosmos. So this, my friend, is a very different state of being than the one you have acquired during your earthly sojourn. You expand into a cosmic consciousness and feel that the world is within you, instead of being in yourself and looking at the world. Does this answer your question, my friend?

Bob: Yes it does Joshua, but I wonder then what 'sense of self' do we have. Do we lose our self-awareness *per se*?

Joshua: No, you don't. This is the peculiar thing, my friend. Although you become expansive, the self-awareness which you have acquired on Earth remains for you. So those religions which suggest that you become a 'non-self' are actually wrong. You grow beyond your earthly self, but your self-awareness nonetheless remains intact, and you know yourself to be a self.

Bob: So does this mean, Joshua, that we retain our sense of individuality, of separateness from others?

Joshua: No, not exactly. Although you retain your self-awareness, you are no longer separate in the sense you experienced on Earth. No, in spirit you merge with others, you interweave with others, you find your being in others, but you know yourself to be a self nonetheless.

Bob: Joshua, some people may find what you are saying contradictory, because on the one hand you say we will have an expanded cosmic consciousness and also merge with others, and yet we still retain a self-conscious awareness. Can we really have both these things co-existing?

Joshua: Yes, my friend, you can, provided you do not close yourself off from others. What do I mean by this? I mean that you still have the possibility to retreat inside yourself, to isolate yourself from the wider spirit world. This can happen if you refuse to extend your love and blessing to the world in which you now live. You can withdraw and, through this, cut yourself off from being a part of the whole cosmos – of the God Being.

Bob: Joshua, I hope I am getting correctly what I think you are saying, that I am receiving your thoughts correctly – am I?

Joshua: Yes you are, my friend, but we do understand that you can have some doubts about this. Don't doubt, my friend, trust in your own abilities.

Bob: Okay Joshua, but what you are describing is certainly unusual for me to think about.

Joshua: Yes, we know it's unusual for you, but if you are to understand spiritual realities, then you need to stretch beyond your usual comfort zone, shall we say.

Bob: Right Joshua, so just to recap. When we die our consciousness expands, and we see ourselves and the world we are in from a different perspective than we are used to, right?

Joshua: Yes, that is correct. Your perception is totally changed. You are now the world, you do not stand facing the world as you did on earth. Now the world is in you and you are the world.

Bob: Right, this is rather mind-bending for me!

Joshua: Good. This means that you are open to consider this as a real possibility, and this possibility is the reality that you grow into, expand into, after your death.

Bob: Is what you have described generally true for all human beings after death, or does it vary from person to person?

Joshua: Well, there is variation, that is true, but what I have described you can take to be the general situation. Of course, it is modified to an extent by the levels of development, spiritually speaking, of those who enter into this spirit world after their earthly deaths.

Bob: So what difference does it make if someone is spiritually aware, shall I say, to someone who is, say, an out and out materialist?

Joshua: Well, in the case of the materialist, it is more difficult for them to let go of their beliefs, their constructs, which they bring over with them when they die. They box themselves in, so to speak, and find it hard to really let themselves go into the new reality. They had no expectation of any form of life or continuation of awareness after death, and this mindset puts them into a sort of prison.

Bob: Can they get out of this?

Joshua: Yes, they can, the moment they let love and light flow towards them and dissolve the mindset that hems them in.

Bob: And where does this love and light come from to release them?

Joshua: It comes from their angels, helped by other higher spirits, who want to lead and guide these souls into the higher dimensions of being.

Bob: Can it take a long time to free a trapped soul?

Joshua: Yes, it can take ages, but it can also sometimes go very quickly. Each case is different and so here we cannot generalise.

Bob: Well Joshua, I think with this I have come as far as I can with this main theme, unless you or the others have anything important to add?

Raja: We would only say to you, my friend, that one question often leads to other questions, but how big do you want to make this book? If you do not want it to grow and grow, then you can leave some questions for another book, perhaps? With this we thank you for doing this work with us, and send our blessings, Raja Lampa.

Bob: Right, thank you everyone.

Commentary

What the guides describe in this chapter regarding what we go through and experience after death, concurs remarkably well with what Rudolf Steiner also conveys to us through his spiritual researches. The panoramic picture of our last Earth-life, followed by the retrospective learning journey through experiencing the effects of our life on others, leading then to sojourns in different regions or spheres of the spirit world, all accord with Steiner's accounts. For example, in transcripts of some of his early lectures entitled, *At the Gates of Spiritual Science*, Steiner says,

> The actual instant of death brings a remarkable experience: for a brief space of time the individuality remembers all that has happened to him in the life just ended. His entire life appears before his soul in a moment, like a great tableau. Something like this can happen during life, in rare moments of great shock or anger – for instance a man who is drowning, or falling from a great height, when death seems imminent, may see his whole life before him in this way.
>
> (Steiner 1970, pp.28-29)

Interestingly, in the same lecture, Steiner then goes on to describe what he refers to as the condition of 'kamaloca' after death. This state consists of a person gradually needing to wean themselves free of their earthly desires, wishes and longings. Although guides do not specifically refer to this particular testing time after death, which has to be suffered through as it were, to my understanding this period also coincides with the retrospective journey when a person must experience how he or she has treated or affected others during their lifetime. Indeed, Steiner refers also to this essential aspect of kamaloca when he later says that,

> During his life a person does not merely do things which yield pleasure; he lives also in the company of other people and other creatures. Consciously or unconsciously, intentionally or unintentionally, he causes pleasure and pain, joy and sorrow, to animals and human beings. All such occasions he will encounter again as he lives through the kamaloca period; he returns to the place and moment when he was the cause of pain to another being. At that time he made someone else feel pain; now he has to suffer the same pain in his own soul.
>
> (Steiner 1970, p.32)

Steiner points out that those who have caused pain and suffering to animals, such as a vivisectionist, whether intentional or not, must themselves experience the suffering they have inflicted.

Only after reliving such events from the point of view of the soul-experiences of others, has a person purified themselves sufficiently of all such earthly effects to be able then to enter into the more spiritual states of Devachan. That is to say into the various regions of the soul and spirit worlds, as described in Steiner's book *Theosophy* (Steiner 1994). This step is also referred to briefly by my guides. In some of Steiner's lectures, specifically those looking at life after death, these regions are also described as the differentiated planetary spheres, through which we travel post mortem.

Actually the so-called kamaloca time is said by Steiner to take place in the Moon-Sphere. Thereafter the spheres or regions of Mercury, Venus, Sun, Mars, Jupiter, Saturn, are traversed as we further expand in our being after death. Beyond these planetary spheres the soul, apparently, then enters into the cosmic realm of the stars *per se* (see Steiner 1975a & 1975b).

However, as I pointed out already in Chapter 3, my purpose in this book is not to make out a case for Steiner's anthroposophy, but to convey the knowledge as given us from my spirit guides. (Those readers who wish to can of course also study Steiner's books and lectures in depth.)

The important matter of meeting our beloved relatives and friends after death is clearly referred to by my guides. In numerous places Steiner certainly affirmed that we remain united with all those with whom we have bonds of love and affection, whether we are in or outside the physical body.

> If we are united with somebody by love, then this love is a seed and one experiences the fruit all through the future, since we belong to such a person throughout the whole future.
>
> (Steiner 1954, p.41)

Moreover, this intimacy is again confirmed when he says that,

> And just as the body, which impedes our sight of the spirit, disappears in the spiritual world, so too in that world every impediment to friendship and love now disappears. Human beings are closer together there than in the flesh.
>
> (Steiner 1963, p.49)

However, our actual awareness of others after death will, it seems, vary according to our own level of spiritual and moral development. In that sense it is important how we prepare ourselves for entering into life after death, whilst still living on the Earth. If a person firmly believes that death marks the end of his or her existence, then when the transition to the afterlife comes about it may, perhaps, not prove to be either easily recognisable or enlightening. However, as the guides pointed out, the essential purpose of our journey after death is to gradually awaken to a realisation of who we really are, not just transient earthly beings, but as truly eternal spirit selves – ideally, to eventually become pure beings of light and love.

References

Steiner, R. (1954) *From the Contents of the Esoteric School (Vol.111).* Anthroposophical Publishing Company, London

Steiner, R. (1963) *The Tension Between East and West.* Hodder and Stoughton

Steiner, R. (1970) *At the Gates of Spiritual Science.* Rudolf Steiner Press

Steiner, R. (1975a) *Life between Death and Rebirth.* Anthroposophic Press

Steiner, R. (1975b) *Between Death and Rebirth.* Rudolf Steiner Press

Steiner, R. (1994) *Theosophy.* Anthroposophic Press (This book is subtitled: *An Introduction to the Spiritual Processes in Human Life and in the Cosmos.*)

6
SPIRIT WORLDS

What Are Spirit Worlds?

In this chapter we will turn to two main interconnecting themes, and there will be a commentary on both of them.

Bob: Joshua, are the guides ready to begin work with me this morning?

Joshua: Yes, my friend, they are. We are all ready and waiting, so to speak, and we look forward to working with you once again.

Bob: Well Joshua, I don't know who wishes to step forward first, to come through and start to give answers to my first main question for this chapter. Who would like to begin, Joshua?

Joshua: Red Cloud wishes to come through and he will do so now.

Red Cloud: Bob, my friend, it is good to work with you once more. In answer to your question let me say the following.

Spirit worlds are regions or dimensions of the universe in which you live. These dimensions interact with the physical dimension in which you live now and where you lead your daily life. However, the spirit worlds, or dimensions of being, fully penetrate your own dimensionality. In this sense they are not separate from you or located in some far reaches of space or time. They are here and now. So this is the first answer to your question, my friend, 'What are spirit worlds?'

However, I will now give you further information. These worlds that you refer to are worlds of vibrations. Now, what do I mean by that? I mean to say that the various dimensions of reality, of spirit reality, are vibrating at various frequencies. They are really 'energy fields', to use a term that is compatible with your understanding of modern science – energy fields in which many different kinds of beings exist side by side. So there are also higher and lower energy fields, and Beings of the appropriate frequency live and exist in those respectively. Now my friend, you may be thinking that this all sounds pretty abstract and theoretical, but actually it isn't. It is the reality of being in which the universe is composed. Matter occupies a low frequency field of energy but spirit levels are higher energy states of being. So, in answer to your overriding question, 'What are spirit worlds?' I have given you the answer that is appropriate for your understanding. Thank you for letting me be the first to contribute today, Red Cloud.

Bob: Thank you, Red Cloud. Joshua, I am learning how to proceed with this work, so perhaps I can try to put further questions and the guides can provide clarifications. Is this a good idea?

Joshua: Shalom, my friend, yes, it is. Simply put your questions and we will see who wishes to step forward.

Bob: Right, Joshua. You say that spirit worlds are actually different dimensions of energy – energy fields. Can someone explain this a bit more, please?

Raja: Yes, I would like to contribute to this, please. When we use the term energy fields we are referring to different levels of states of being. You see, everything consists of energy, the energy of love and light. Love and light are the core substances that create the universe in which we all exist. Love and light are not simply abstractions of some sort but real, objective you could say, substances, which emanate from the Creator being of the world – of the cosmos. We realise that this may be difficult to grasp with your ordinary, day-to-day consciousness, but nonetheless it is true. The whole universe, the cosmos, is composed of love and light as the basic substances, forces, energies, which create all that is. So in answer to your question, my friend, they are worlds of love and light in every respect.

Bob: Well, Raja Lampa, this can sound rather simplistic, can't it, when as human beings we think of the universe, and multiverses, as described by modern cosmologists and physicists? I don't think they would be able to accept your explanation!

Raja: No, my friend, perhaps not, but nonetheless this is the truth of the matter. Love and light are the forces which build the universe and build the different energy fields which make up the totality of the cosmos.

Bob: Okay, so can I ask further questions now which belong, I think, under my main umbrella question, so to speak?

Pierre: Yes, my friend, you can.

Bob: So what do spirit worlds look like? I mean do they have mountains, lakes, seas, plains, cliffs, deserts, etc., somehow like we do on Earth, or is it all very different from what we know down here?

Pierre: My friend, it is very different. On Earth, that is to say in the material dimension of existence, you have all the topographical features set out before you in clear, concrete, definite forms. This is not the case in higher dimensions of reality. Instead of fixed, definite forms and structures, everything is in movement; it is mobile and fluidic, compared to the denseness of your earthly existence. Energy flows – it is not fixed down in definite forms. So this is a basic, fundamental difference, my friend, between your world on the earthly plane of being and our worlds in the higher dimensions. Life flows, love flows, light flows. It is not stuck and static.

Bob: Alright, I can somehow see that. It gives a very dynamic picture, but still if there aren't any mountains, valleys, seas, rivers, plains and pastures, then what is there to walk through or stand on, or sail through for that matter?

Philip: May I step in now? You see, my friend and brother, you cannot really compare your physical world to the worlds of spirit beings. And I deliberately say spirit beings, because these worlds are worlds of beings, living beings. Nothing is dead in the spirit worlds, nothing is without life and movement. Yes, it is true to say that some beings are more lively than others. Some are more quiescent but, compared to what you know on Earth, ours is a universe of ceaseless activity and change and metamorphosis. What do I mean by metamorphosis? I mean that beings are constantly changing their forms, their appearances, but not in any chaotic ways, but rather according to organic, living, laws of being.

Bob: Philip, may I stop you there please. Now I'm getting quite confused. So Philip, I believe that when we die on Earth we leave our physical bodies and enter into spirit worlds – am I correct in thinking this?

Philip: Yes, my friend and brother, you are quite correct in thinking that.

Bob: Okay Philip, so are you then saying that I will lose my form, that I will be metamorphosing myself in spirit worlds?

Philip: Yes, my friend, I am saying that but remember this is all part of a process of development for you as a human being. As a human being you are following a particular line of evolution, so to speak. Not all beings are following the same lines as you, so what applies to the human experience in terms of soul and spirit, differs from, say, how that is for me as an angel being, or how that is for an elemental being. We have to differentiate different lines, or ways, of evolving ever upwards.

Bob: So Philip, we are all living in an evolving universe, is that right?

Philip: Yes, my friend, and brother we are. Nothing is standing still, all is on a path or paths of progression and development.

Bob: Even with angels, archangels, cherubim, seraphim, etc.?

Philip: Yes, even with all those various levels of being. The universe evolves and all the beings contained within it evolve also. It is dynamic, vibrant, multi-dimensional and ever changing.

Bob: Thank you, Philip, that's quite a picture you paint! Let me ask another question. Are there any definite, recognisable features of spirit worlds – I mean 'landmarks', or something which enables us to know where we are at any time?

Markos: Let me step in please with this question. There are no landmarks in the way that you imagine them. Imagine them, that is, in comparison with the landmarks that are found throughout the earthly world. No Himalayas, no Rocky Mountains, no Pacific ocean, no Sahara desert. None of these in any recognisable form for your spirit senses. However, there are differentiations to be found. Not everything is just homogenous and sameness. In fact, there is a vast amount of differentiation. It is expressed in colours, sounds, movements and music. It is a melody here, a symphony there, a light play over there, a spectrum of colours not found in the earthly dimension.

Bob: Okay, so how do spirits find their way around in all this? Where are the route maps?

Markos: We don't have route maps as on Earth, but we do have guides who will show us the way to go; guides who are beings of greater wisdom than ourselves, guides who move from above to below to help us find the direction of travel to move in. The direction that is most appropriate for us at any given time, though time is not really a reality for us here. We move and have our being in a state of timelessness, in a state of perpetual presence.

Bob: Thank you Markos, by now my mind is certainly having trouble to cope with all these other-world descriptions. I will try to find one or two questions to bring this session to a close. Is there a certain hierarchy of being in the spirit, I mean a sort of ordered structure of some sort? Otherwise all this dynamic movement sounds pretty chaotic to me.

Pan: My friend, you are treading into new realms of being so you can't expect it to be just like you're used to! But in answer to your last question, yes there is order and structure, in a free and dynamic way. There are different levels, states, worlds, of beingness. Beings belong in one or another of these levels for a time, but when I say 'time', this is just to give you something to hold on to. It is a knowing when a passing from one energy level to another is possible – is necessary. The universe is ordered, it is not really chaotic, but it may appear so to your human level of understanding. The more you get to know the spirit worlds, the more you will see that there is clear order and structure, but in a divine rather than a human sense.

Bob: Okay Pan, but one last question please. Are there really many worlds – spirit worlds – or is it really all one world with many parts to it?

Pan: Yes, it is really one world, you are right in this but this one world has many dimensions within it. This is what you can refer to as 'spirit worlds'. So, a oneness in diversity, or a diversity in oneness. Hope this is clear to you?

Bob: Well, as clear as it is going to be for today, I think. Thank you everyone. Joshua, when I have had time to look at this I will have to see whether we have another session on this theme, or pass on to the next question. At the moment I am not sure about this.

Joshua: That is alright, my friend. You are having to take in a lot of new ideas so be kind to yourself! All blessings, Joshua Isaiah.

*

Bob: Joshua, this is now the second session continuing the theme from yesterday, namely, 'What are spirit worlds?' Is this alright with yourself and the other guides?

Joshua: Shalom, my friend. Yes, it is perfectly alright. We are waiting in the wings, so to speak, to work with you on this theme.

Bob: Right Joshua, so I will start to put some further questions since reading what I received yesterday. You speak of spirit worlds as energy fields or as dimensions of reality. How many different or interweaving dimensions are we talking about, or, I suppose I could say, how many spirit worlds are there? I will just be open to see who wants to answer this one.

Markos: I will try to answer your question, my friend. As regards the number of dimensions, we could say that they are countless. That is to say, a very great number of different dimensions are to be found. I cannot put any exact number on this.

Bob: Well Markos, if I just go with my wish, shall I say, to have a manageable number, I would probably have asked you if there are twelve dimensions – a sort of cosmic number – twelve constellations of the Zodiac, etc. What do you think of that?

Markos: Well my friend, you might like to think like that, but this doesn't accord with the actual reality! There are many, many, dimensions, or, if you like, spirit worlds.

Bob: Markos yesterday Pan told me that really there is one world, but that within that world there are many dimensions or spirit worlds. Is that right?

Markos: Yes, it is absolutely right, my friend. *'In my Father's house are many mansions'*, to quote from the Bible. This is a true picture of the reality. One house, but many mansions, or dimensions, or worlds.

Bob: Okay, so I will go with that, but then is it meaningful for me to ask what the spirit worlds are like, since there are so many of them?

Pierre: Let me step in here, please. It is meaningful, in the sense that you want to have some understanding of them. However, to try to compare them to your usual earthly experiences is rather difficult, if not impossible.

Bob: Yes Pierre, but without some sort of comparison, how can I or others form any concepts of what they are like?

Pierre: Well, that is just the problem. They are other-worldly in comparison to earth life.

Bob: So what do you suggest then?

Pierre: We suggest that you try to live into the descriptions that we can give to you, in the language we are using.

Bob: Okay, if I go with that then, so far spirit worlds have been described as mobile, dynamic, ever-changing, and composed of love and light. Is that right?

Pierre: Yes, that is correct. In that sense it is like living in an ever-changing kaleidoscope of colours, sounds, music, scents, tastes etc.

Bob: This sounds to me like living in a sea of sensations.

Pierre: Yes, it is very much like that, but it also depends on which level you are looking at.

Bob: Do you mean that this varies or is different at different levels or states of being?

Pierre: Precisely. It is like a spectrum of levels or frequencies of energies, and so your experiences will depend on which level you find yourself in.

Bob: Right. Let me ask another question. According to Rudolf Steiner's book *Theosophy* there are so-called 'soul worlds' as well as 'spirit worlds'. That is, Steiner differentiates the soul world as such from the spirit world, I think when he is talking about the journey of a human being after death. So are there soul worlds *per se*?

Philip: I will step in here, please. Yes we know what Steiner is referring to. He is again talking about different levels and dimensions of spirit experiences. So yes, if he chooses to call them soul worlds, then that is fine, but it is included in the descriptions we have so far given you.

Bob: Alright Philip, but if I remember rightly, I think Steiner talks about maybe seven levels in the soul world and seven levels in the spirit world. Now, that together would make, say, fourteen different levels. This is a lot less than the 'countless' dimensions that Markos talked about.

Philip: Yes, my friend and brother, you are right in saying this, but remember Steiner only talked about the levels that he did as a first introduction to these realms. He had to keep it manageable for his readers. He knew, he knows, that there are many, many more levels which he could not then enter into in his descriptions. It would have been too much for people to take in.

Bob: Well, I can certainly understand that! So let me ask please, what else can you tell me, Philip, about 'What are spirit worlds?' that would either add to what I have been told so far, or else clarify that further?

Philip: Well, my friend and brother, we have actually told you the essence of this already. We have described that love and light are the key substances, or forces or energies from which all these dimensions are made. We have also told you of the dynamic, ever-changing, nature of these worlds or dimensions. If you want to know exactly what they look like, then this means you are still imagining them compared to your earthly reality, but this is actually not a valid comparison because they are so totally different. Remember, my friend and brother, that these worlds are really the 'places' where beings live. It is a world of *beinghood*, not a world of matter.

Bob: Well Philip, this would also lead me into another main theme that also belongs to this chapter, namely, 'Who lives in spirit worlds?' Should we start to look at that question now?

Philip: Yes, we can do so if you want to, but we are also aware that your hand is feeling tired with all the writing you do, so perhaps we should tackle this theme tomorrow?

Bob: Yes, Philip and everyone else, I agree. I will stop for today. Many thanks for working with me.

Philip: You are most welcome.

Bob: Joshua, just to check. Is this alright if I stop here and then look at that main question next time?

Joshua: Of course it is. We are working with you, but it is you who needs to take the initiative and judge what you can manage. All blessings, Joshua.

Bob: Thank you.

*

(In this next session I did however continue with my first theme.)

Bob: Joshua, on the theme of 'What are Spirit Worlds?' and based on the descriptions given to me, many people may feel that they don't sound very inviting! They might think, 'I don't really want to go there after I die'. What would you say to this?

Joshua: Shalom, my friend. Yes, I understand what you are asking, and I also understand that some people, perhaps many, may not be enamoured by what we have said. But remember my friend, we are talking about worlds of energy and worlds of beings. These worlds have a different character and consistency from what you know in your material, physical existence. They cannot be compared with your usual sensory experiences and, therefore, they must be viewed in a different light altogether.

Bob: Yes Joshua, I can accept that but basically people would want to know if these worlds are friendly? Are they nice, pleasant places to be in, or should people feel afraid of them?

Joshua: No, people should not fear them, they are not threatening in any way, provided of course that a person during their earthly life has not created their own hell, so to speak.

Bob: What do you mean by that?

Joshua: I mean that if they have done evil deeds or led a debased sort of life, then they will find themselves in the place after death where they will suffer the consequences of their actions.

Bob: So does hell exist?

Joshua: Shalom, my friend, yes it does for those who have created it themselves in life.

Bob: And for the others? Those that have tried to live decent lives and treated other people fairly? How is that, where do they find themselves after death?

Joshua: Well, they will find themselves exactly where they have prepared the environment during their earthly lives. They will be surrounded by the situation which they themselves have created.

Bob: So are you saying, Joshua, that we ourselves are creating spirit worlds, or at least places in these worlds for ourselves by our lives on Earth?

Joshua: Yes, I am saying precisely that. You yourselves create your own environments, your 'mansions', to live in after your deaths on Earth. It is entirely of your own making.

Bob: In that sense are there as many worlds as there are human beings who create them?

Joshua: Yes there are, though there are many common areas, so to speak. Areas where souls or spirits with similar outlooks will gather and share in their surroundings.

Bob: So it is not entirely individual and separate then?

Joshua: No, it's not. It is where you with others of like mind will gravitate towards, where you will find yourselves together.

Bob: So, just coming back to this point then. Are spirit worlds happy worlds for us to be in? Are they pleasurable?

Joshua: They can be, certainly. Again, it all depends how you have prepared yourselves to enter into them during your earthly lives.

Bob: Well Joshua, this does make it sound better than some people might have thought – not just vibrations and energies, but also some enjoyments?

Joshua: Yes certainly, this is so, but remember you have created your place to be during your lives, so this also means you can construct a happy or a miserable existence for yourselves after death when you move into spirit.

Bob: Well then, yes, it is important to know what we are doing, not so?

Joshua: Yes, it is very important to realise what you are creating every day of your lives.

Bob: Is there anything further you would wish to add, Joshua?

Joshua: No, my friend. We have answered your questions and we hope that this has given you, and our readers, pause for thought and reflection. All blessings, Joshua.

Bob: Thank you, Joshua.

Commentary

It is interesting how, so far in this chapter, the guides are attempting to describe the nature of spirit worlds, given that they are very 'other-wordly' compared to our everyday life on Earth. Whereas we live here in a world of things – solid things like houses, cars, computers, cups and saucers, etc. – those in spirit live fundamentally in worlds of beings. Yes, we also have other people with and around us, as well as various animals and plants, depending on just where we live geographically, but all these things have definite forms as part of their material manifestations. While it is true that these various forms do change over time, even in the solid kingdom of the minerals, still this has nothing like the lively dynamism and mobile, metamorphosing characteristics which belong, it seems, to the spirit worlds.

The guides say that these are worlds of 'energy-fields', vibrating at various frequencies and comprising a multitude of interpenetrating regions or dimensions. However, the essential basic substances, so to speak, are described as love and light. Do any of these spirit world characteristics find resonances in the published spiritual-scientific researches of Rudolf Seiner? In his seminal book *Theosophy*, Steiner endeavours to help us gain some understanding for the differentiated regions of, firstly, the 'soul world', and then also the 'spirit world', *per se*. Whilst it is obviously best to read and live with Steiner's own descriptions, the question for us here is whether they are the same, or similar, to what the guides have communicated to us. Well, at first sight they do appear to be rather dissimilar, both in the terminology used to depict them and also in the substance of their contents. Steiner certainly does not speak of energy-fields or of levels of vibrations or frequencies. It is interesting however that when two writers who recently drew upon Steiner's findings, are describing the higher spiritual worlds (or Devachan) they express themselves thus:

> For example, Rudolf Steiner pointed out that this world is made of a 'material' of which human thought consists. It is a world of living thoughts, or spiritual beings. These living thoughts or spiritual beings have also been referred to as archetypes, for example, by Plato.

They then add that:

> The archetypes are energy, vibration, and sound. They manifest as a purely spiritual phenomenon which cannot be compared to the sounds we hear in the physical world. The beings of the spiritual world express themselves in this spiritual vibration, this sea of sound.
>
> (Brink and Stolp 2017, p.68)

When speaking of the soul world, in contrast to devachan, Steiner himself distinguishes two basic forces, which he says may be called *sympathy* and *antipathy*.

> Sympathy is the force with which soul formations attract each other, try to merge with each other, and let their affinity take effect. Antipathy, on the other hand, is the force through which soul formations repel and exclude each other, and

> maintain their own identity. The role a soul formation plays in the soul world depends on the extent to which these basic forces are present in it.
>
> (Steiner 1994, p.103)

These various formations, differentiated according to the measures of sympathy and antipathy within them, constitute the seven different regions of this world, through which the human being journeys after death. This is also the passage through the state of kamaloca referred to previously, by which the human being becomes ever freer of earthly desires and ties. It is therefore an upward journey of purification, as preparation for entering into the spirit world *per se*, or devachan, which Steiner describes in *Theosophy* as 'The Country of Spirit Beings'. Of this new territory he writes the following,

> This is the world of the spirit, and it is so different from the physical world that everything we have to say about it will seem sheer fantasy to those willing to trust only their physical senses. We had to use comparisons and imagery to describe the soul world, and that is even more the case here.

And a little later,

> It must be emphasised above all that this spiritual world is woven out of the substance that constitutes human thought – 'substance' in a very figurative sense, of course.
>
> (Steiner 1994, pp.122-123)

He makes it clear, however, that human thoughts are like shadows compared to the *living* thoughts or spirit beings to be found in these non-physical dimensions, wherein live the spiritual archetypes of all the things and beings that exist in the physical and soul worlds.

Steiner also points out that,

> In the spiritual world, everything is in constant activity, constant motion, constant creation.
>
> (Steiner 1994, p.124)

He goes on to describe seven regions of the spirit world, as he did earlier with the soul world. Although Steiner's account is much more detailed and differentiated, and expressed differently than what the guides have communicated to us so far, nonetheless I think there are some clear parallels to be found. The mobility and flowing nature of spirit worlds, worlds of beings, spiritual colours, sounds, music, etc. Essentially, the guides have presented us with a brief, rather broad and general account, whereas Steiner goes into greater details. Interestingly, in a course of lectures to do with 'the manifestations of karma', Steiner refers to love and light as being the fundamental forces of our existence.

> Love and light are the two elements, the two components, which permeate all earthly existence : love as the soul constituent of earthly being, light as the outer material constituent of earthly being.
>
> (Steiner 1995a, p.161)

If this is the fundamental reality behind all of our earthly existence, then it is not too difficult to imagine, as the guides tell us, that the whole universe, the cosmos, is composed of love and light as the basic substances, forces, energies, that create all that is.

References

Brink van den, M. and Stolp, H. (2017) *What Happens When We Die – Our Journey in the Afterlife.* Temple Lodge Publishing

Steiner, R. (1994) *Theosophy.* Anthroposophic Press

Steiner, R. (1995a) *Manifestations of Karma.* Rudolf Steiner Press

Who Lives There?

Having considered the 'what are' of spirit worlds, we now go on to explore their 'inhabitants'. Both these themes clearly belong intimately together in these spiritual dimensions, and therefore also in this chapter.

Bob: So Joshua, I want to start this session now and turn to the question of, 'Who lives there?' – that is, in spirit worlds. Is this alright with you and the other guides?

Joshua: Shalom, my friend. Yes, it is perfectly alright with us. Let us see who would first like to step forward to answer your question.

Bob: Okay.

Red Cloud: May I start with this today? As you know, my friend, in my previous incarnation I was a Chief of the Sioux. In those days we – the Native Americans I mean – had a direct connection with worlds of spirit. We felt a natural affinity with those realms of existence that are standing behind, as it were, the outer physical existence. And so it was that we could appeal to those beings who lived in spirit worlds – in spirit – to help us with our earthly, daily lives. Of course my friend, you also know that there were other cultures in the past, let us say the Egyptian culture, which spanned many thousands of years, in which people on Earth appealed to those in spirit to help and guide them in their earthly lives. Now my friend, to turn specifically to your question, your second main question for this chapter, 'Who lives in spirit worlds?' I would say the following.

Many different types of beings live in these worlds; in these different dimensions of reality. You know some of these beings from religious doctrines, shall we say, or from other esoteric sources. I mean the beings referred to as angels, archangels, archai, etc. – names that you are familiar with. In short my friend, a whole host of beings inhabit the dimensions or levels of spirit – call them spirit worlds. These beings are following their particular paths of evolution and development, because all beings are evolving, nothing is static and stationary, all is in constant movement and progression. Such is the universe in which we all live. So my friend, this gives you a certain picture – and now I will let someone else step forward and make their contributions. All blessings, Red Cloud.

Bob: Thank you, Red Cloud. Can I ask for further information about who lives in spirit worlds, let us say how is it with us human beings?

Markos: Well my friend, with human beings it is a question of consciousness and states of development. What do I mean by this? I mean, my friend, that all human beings will live in spirit worlds, in a sense do so continuously, but how aware they are of where they are living and how they are living there, can vary enormously. It depends on how far they have come in their own evolutionary development. In other words, my friend, some people in spirit are wide-awake and aware, whilst others are stumbling along in a state of semi-sleep.

Bob: Well, this is interesting, very interesting, in fact. Can you say more about this please?

Markos: Yes, I can. You see my friend, not all human beings are the same. This is of course obvious to you. People stand at different levels of awareness, even in their ordinary daily lives. Some people muddle through life, giving little thought to what they are doing or why they are doing it. Other people are extremely aware and awake to every action they take and give thought to the affairs of life and their relationships with others, etc. So there is a great difference, or great differences, to be found amongst those who dwell on the earth-plane. It is the variety of life, so to speak. But depending on the inner awareness, the self-awareness, also the spiritual awareness of people – so they will live, do live, in spirit worlds in different states of awareness and at different levels of being.

Bob: Yes Markos, I can understand this. This makes perfect sense I would say, but how then, for example, do human beings in spirit relate to other beings who are not human?

Pierre: May I step in here? This is an interesting question and one with which I have also occupied myself, also living here in spirit. Why? Because it is a constant challenge to see how best to relate to those whom one meets in these spirit realms. To see how to work with them, learn with them, socialise with them, in ways that are compatible with the divine laws in which we live and move in these higher dimensions of existence. How, let me say, to work with the angels so that we can help to bring harmony and peace into the Earth sphere? Or how to work with cherubim – that is, very high spirit beings who are closer to the Creator being, and who also wish to help human beings make progress in their evolution? You see what I mean, my friend? We can start to see how to relate to beings of all different levels and ranks, and so create a new harmony and togetherness.

Bob: Well Pierre, I can to an extent understand what you mean, but it seems a big jump from angels to cherubim!

Pierre: Yes, it is a big jump, but remember that all beings are in service to God, to the Creator being of the universe. Therefore they all wish to cooperate in bringing about harmony and peace, especially when they view the chaos which human beings are bringing about on the Earth! There is much to be done to try to restore balance and harmony when free will allows chaos and disruption to proliferate!

Bob: Yes, I can see this. What about other sorts of beings, for example I am thinking now of the elementals and the nature spirits? Do they also belong, live, in spirit worlds?

Raja: Yes, they do. They live in spirit worlds but like many other beings they also have a field of action on the earth-plane. Their true home is in spirit, as also is the true home of all human beings, but like human beings they have the task to uphold the Earth planet as the home for earthly lives to run their course. The Earth is indeed a special place, it has a certain uniqueness, and therefore it is the field of action for many beings to work there and to gradually bring about a transformation to a more spiritual state of existence.

Bob: Yes, I can understand that because I believe the planet, the Earth, is meant to evolve also, just as we are. Am I right in this?

Raja: Yes, my friend, you are right in this. The Earth is meant to become ever more spiritualised, in the sense that the denser vibrations which create your normal physical realities are to be raised into higher and lighter frequencies of being. This is what I mean by spiritualisation. An overcoming of the denseness of physical matter, though bear in mind that even physical matter is really a form of energy operating at a lower level of existence. All is energy, all is spirit, and in that sense what you call 'matter' is really an illusion, a non-entity in fact.

Bob: Raja, this gets me at least into tricky conceptual grounds! Can we come back to *who* exactly lives in spirit worlds please?

Raja: Yes, we can. My fellow guides have already explained or described to you that there are myriad beings, you could say, who live in these higher dimensional worlds. These beings are creative in following divine laws, and I say laws because there really are laws, rules, which govern the whole universe. Nothing is arbitrary or by chance, as you would say. Everything follows divine order and discipline. It is only human beings who with their free will can wreak chaos and havoc on Earth, and even cause some disruption in spirit worlds when they bring their strong emotions and confused thoughts with them here. This takes time, so to speak, to unravel and to bring about an awareness of how they need to transform themselves.

Bob: But Raja, I thought that human beings are essentially spirit beings themselves?

Raja: Yes, they are, but often completely unaware of their own true natures! And this is when trouble ensues. It is a process of helping human beings to recognise who they truly are, and this can be quite a challenge!

Bob: Another question, please. It is not only human beings that live on Earth, but we share the planet with animals and plants, birds and fishes, etc. Do they have any reality in the spirit worlds? I mean, do they somehow live there too?

Raja: Yes, they do, but not in the forms in which they appear on the earth-plane. Their essential beings live in higher dimensions but, as with human beings, their reflections, so to speak, dwell on the physical, material level.

Bob: So can we see plants and animals in the spirit worlds?

Raja: Yes you can, if you recognise them for who they really are.

Bob: How do we do that?

Raja: By getting behind their physical appearances and relating yourselves to their spirit essences.

Bob: I think I should soon draw to a close; is there anyone else who wishes to contribute still?

Joshua: Yes, let me bring our session to a close. You see my friend that the guides are more than willing to help you shed light on your questions. This is something important for you to convey to others, because you cannot hope to fathom the many questions of your existence on Earth without reference to the spirit that stands behind everything. And I do mean everything. Nothing exists except that it has its real being in spirit. In that sense the spirit worlds stand behind, underlie, and are the foundation of your earthly existence, indeed of the Earth planet *per se*.
So what you are attempting to convey in your new book is not for nothing. It is actually of great importance, even though many will not yet be able to accept it. So well done, my friend, for your efforts to do this. We will continue to help you in this endeavour. All blessings, Joshua Isaiah.

Bob: Thank you, Joshua and everyone else.

*

Bob: Joshua, I would like to ask further questions on this main theme. Is that alright with you?

Joshua: Shalom, my friend. Yes, it is perfectly alright, we look forward to being of help to you in your writing.

Bob: So Joshua, for whoever wishes to step forward, my question is this. A main theme in Rudolf Steiner's work is that there are, let's call them adversary beings or spirits, living in the spirit worlds, who oppose the rightful evolution of human beings. He refers to them as the luciferic and ahrimanic beings. Do you and the guides know who he is referring to? Does this make sense to you?

Markos: I would like to pick this up, please. Yes, we do know what and who Rudolf Steiner was referring to. He is quite right to point out the need to have awareness of these particular beings. They are indeed spiritual beings who work actively to mislead human beings and to influence them in ways that impede their forward progress.

Bob: Well yes, that is what I understand. Steiner said that the luciferic beings increase our pride and egotism, whereas the ahrimanic beings breed fear and materialism into us. Or that is how I would briefly put what I understand from him.

Markos: Yes, my friend, that is a good way of characterising their particular qualities, shall we say. At any event they do act against the course of human evolution and yet, on the other hand, they also enhance that evolution through their influences on the human being.

Bob: Isn't what you say contradictory?

Markos: Yes, it appears to be so, but in reality, it isn't. You grow in strength precisely because there are forces, or beings of opposition, to increase your own forces, provided of course you are aware of what their game is. If you are aware of them then you can channel their influences to your own advantage. However, ignorance is bliss they say, and that is the state these beings would like human beings to be in – blissful ignorance!

Bob: So when Steiner makes such a point of describing them again and again, he is trying to wake us up out of our blissful ignorance?

Markos: Indeed he is, but unfortunately this is a difficult thing to do. It depends on people really wanting to acquire genuine self-knowledge and very many people just do not want this at all. They would rather live in illusions about their own goodness and greatness, shall I say, than realise how flawed they can be, are, in many respects.

Bob: So these adversary beings do live, then, in spirit worlds – is that right?

Markos: Yes, they do indeed and we do have an awareness of them. Nonetheless it is better to focus on those many beings who are endeavouring to support the rightful course of human and planetary evolution, rather than spend too much time thinking about negative influences. As you know, my friend, like attracts like, and so it is far better to attract to yourself the influences, the beings, who can help you in the most positive ways.

Bob: Yes, I see that, but isn't it true to say that both the luciferic and ahrimanic beings do help us in various ways also?

Markos: Well yes, they do, but they don't mean to! It is rather that the wise guidance of mankind has seen to it that, in spite of their own efforts, these beings can somehow contribute positive things as well as negative.

Bob: And I imagine that very much depends on the consciousness and awareness of human beings?

Markos: Yes, it does. Those who are aware can utilise the influences of these beings to their own advantage. However, people who are oblivious of them do stand in real danger of being led astray.

Bob: In what part of the spirit world or worlds are these beings to be found? Do they occupy particular parts, regions, or are they everywhere?

Markos: They are in fact everywhere. They spread their influence throughout the spirit worlds and, in that sense, are pervasive. But on the other hand they are also confined within certain limits.

Bob: Okay Markos, now this sounds quite contradictory. They can't be everywhere and also confined, can they?

Markos: Well in fact they can. Yes, it appears to be a contradiction but, in fact, it isn't. Their influence is widespread but it is nonetheless limited. They are only allowed so much leeway, shall we say, to pursue their objectives. Beyond certain limits they are curtailed and held in check.

Bob: By whom?

Markos: By the wise spirits who oversee the progression of the world, of the cosmos. Remember, nothing is arbitrary; everything is subject to divine law.

Bob: Right Markos, well this sounds reassuring but perhaps this is as far as we will go for now.

Markos: Yes, if you feel that is enough for now, then we can stop. All blessings, Markos.

*

Bob: Joshua, I still have a few more questions on this theme. Can we turn to these this morning?

Joshua: Shalom, my friend. Yes, we can, and we will see who wishes to step forward to answer them.

Bob: Right. Steiner, and of course the Christian tradition also, speak of nine distinct ranks or hierarchies of spirit beings, going from the angels right up to the cherubim and seraphim. Is this correct? Do such ranks or levels of development of beings exist in the spirit worlds?

Red Cloud: Yes, they do, my friend. There is order and harmony in the spirit worlds. Beings exist on all different levels and contribute to the harmony of the universe. There are those who are closest to man, to humankind, and there are those who are closest to God – to the Creator being of the universe or cosmos.

Bob: So there are definite ranks, or orders, of beings. Correct?

Red Cloud: Yes, that is correct. Each order, or rank, has its role to play within the life of the whole universe. Each performs its functions and tasks according to the Divine Laws.

Bob: So where do the different ranks of beings live; have they got designated areas to inhabit?

Red Cloud: No, not in the sense that you mean. There are no boundaries, no designated regions, as you have on Earth as borders and boundaries. But there are understandings, shall I say, as to where are the legitimate fields of activity of the different beings within the whole cosmos.

Bob: Right. Can I now ask another question please, and this concerns the cosmic Christ. Am I right in thinking that this being, who once lived on Earth in Jesus, is also to be found in the spirit worlds?

Red Cloud: Yes, you are right in thinking this. He is the Lord of Life and his light pervades the spirit worlds and illumines all beings who are drawn towards him.

Bob: Aren't then all beings drawn to him?

Red Cloud: No, not all. Those beings who deliberately turn away from his light and love prefer to live in the darkness and pursue their own aims.

Bob: Would this also apply to human beings who live in spirit?

Red Cloud: It can do, but in the vast majority of cases human beings are drawn towards the light of the cosmic Christ and wish to receive what he can give to them.

Bob: Wouldn't all human beings wish to do that?

Red Cloud: No, not all. Those that practice meanness and are full of hate and fear turn away from the light of Christ and stay in their own places of spirit existence.

Bob: But isn't the aim that all would be saved, so to speak, redeemed, and led onwards?

Red Cloud: Yes, ideally that is so, but still it does require that each soul comes to that clarity for itself. There is still free will in the spirit for human beings.

Bob: Actually I feel that this has now answered all that I wish to ask. So thank you, Red Cloud.

Red Cloud: Thank you, my friend. All blessings, Red Cloud.

Commentary

It is good to just remind ourselves that the knowledge of spirit worlds given by my guides in this book is meant to be accessible for general readers. That is to say, for ordinary people – though we could also say that, spiritually, everyone is extraordinary! – who wonder if there is such a thing as an afterlife and, if so, where and what that new existence is like for us. Therefore, this book does not go into anything like the detailed and comprehensive esoteric research findings we find in Steiner's anthroposophy. Nonetheless, in the commentaries we are trying to see if there is at least broad agreement between what Steiner said and what the guides have given us.

Clearly, the spirit worlds and the cosmos, from the guides' accounts, are inhabited, populated, by a whole range of spirit beings standing at various levels of evolutionary development. This is also very much confirmed in Steiner's work.

> An essential aspect of becoming accustomed to the suprasensory worlds is the realisation that, in place of the states and characteristics that surround our consciousness in the sensory world, there are beings. The suprasensory world is revealed, finally, as a world of beings. Aside from those beings, everything else that exists there is the expression of their deeds. Furthermore, the sensory and elemental worlds also appear as the deeds of those beings.
>
> (Steiner 1999a, p.74)

In Steiner's anthroposophy, as has already been mentioned, there are different regions, or spheres, of supersensible existence, with correspondingly varied spirit inhabitants. The guides' inclusion of, for example, so-called elemental beings (or nature spirits) and higher hierarchical beings (the angels upwards) within the spirit worlds, together with discarnate human beings is, overall, in keeping with Steiner's more specific investigations. From our very human point of view the following observation concerning who lives in spirit worlds is especially pertinent.

> The people with whom we lived in the physical world are encountered again in the spiritual world. Just as everything that the soul once possessed through the physical body falls away, so does the bond that once linked soul to soul in physical life free itself from the circumstances that only had meaning and reality in the physical world. But what one soul was to another in physical life lives on after death, lives on in the spiritual world. Of course words coined to describe physical circumstances can only inexactly express what takes place in the spiritual world. Taking this into account, however, it is certainly correct to say that souls who belonged together during physical life meet again in the spiritual world and continue their lives together under the circumstances of that world.
>
> (Steiner 1994, p.137)

We will hear more from the guides about such close human links in later chapters. Their acknowledgement of the reality and roles of the so-called luciferic and ahrimanic spirit beings is significant, certainly given the emphasis which Steiner places upon them in the course of world evolution (see Steiner 1997). However, we are reassured that they have to act within the limitations imposed upon them by divine law. Finally, the answer to my questions concerning the cosmic Christ also tally with my understanding of the central role ascribed to Christ in Steiner's anthroposophy. In a very real sense, the cosmic being we call 'Christ' in the Christian tradition can be our ultimate guide both in the earthly and the spirit worlds, leading us to realise who we truly are as spirit beings.

References

Steiner, R. (1994) *Theosophy*. Anthroposophic Press
Steiner, R. (1997) *An Outline of Esoteric Science.* Anthroposophic Press
Steiner, R. (1999a) *A Way of Self-Knowledge.* Anthroposophic Press

7
WHERE WE LIVE

Where We Live There

Bob: So, Joshua and everyone else, I want to turn now to the theme of, 'Where do we live in spirit worlds?' In a sense, this is quite a wide theme, because it can encompass quite a lot of different areas. I mean, for example, if we compare it now with our earthly lives. We live in houses of some sort, but we also live in a particular area or neighbourhood, a particular country, a particular landscape, climate, cultural milieu, etc. There are many different layers of where we live on Earth. Having said that, I want to ask some quite fundamental, naive questions, you could say. Questions that ordinary people – I mean not highly-intellectual people – might well ask. So, can we start this session today.

Joshua: Shalom, my friend. Yes, we can. We are ready to help you gain clarity over this question.

Bob: Okay. So on Earth we live in houses of some sort, be they council houses or mansions. Somehow, we have a roof over our heads to protect us from the elements. When we pass to spirit do we live in a house?

Markos: No my friend, not in a house as you know it on Earth. Not in a solid substantial structure, but you do live in a dwelling place. That will be the place you have created for yourself whilst you lived your earthly life. You will migrate, so to speak, to that place, that situation, which represents what you yourself have chosen.

Bob: Okay, so does that mean that if I have chosen to live in a country cottage by the sea, that is where I will find myself after death?

Markos: Not exactly. Yes, if a country cottage by the sea is your greatest wish, then that desire will create the illusion of you living in that situation. It is where you will feel at home, to begin with at least.

Bob: But you say it is an illusion. So does that mean it is not really real?

Markos: It is very real to your experience, your soul experience, but it has no greater reality than what you have made of it.

Bob: So are you saying, Markos, that we find ourselves living in those 'places' or situations which we desire, wish, to find ourselves in?

Markos: Yes, initially, that is exactly it. You find yourselves in the setting, the environment, that you wish to be in.

Bob: But it is really an illusion, a sort of dream perhaps?

Markos: Well yes, but a living dream, a substantial dream compared to your normal sort of dreams when you are in the physical body.

Bob: Nonetheless Markos, it is a dream, my fantasy, my own wished-for illusion.

Markos: Not quite, my friend. Your ideas of reality and illusion are determined by your earthly experiences. In the realm that you pass to after death, it is not so black and white. Your illusions have their own reality, their own validity, you could say.

Bob: Okay Markos, so does everyone after death find themselves in their own place, their own sort of house, you could say, depending upon what they wish for or perhaps expect to be?

Markos: Yes, this is pretty much it. You are correct with that. Each person will find themselves, to begin with, where they wish themselves to be.

Bob: Markos, you say 'to begin with', so does this change; does it move on to something else?

Markos: Yes it does. It moves on into a more objective reality, you could say, in the sense that it is no longer just your own personal creation. You find a place which you can share and be in with others.

Bob: Alright Markos, this was anticipating my further question, because I wondered whether we were each alone living in our house or dwelling, or if we were together with others, like our family and friends?

Markos: Well you have already met some of your family and friends, but they have been in spirit longer than you and have had more time to find themselves there. You are just starting out, if now we imagine you have only just died.

Bob: So are you saying that I start off in my own place and then join with others at their places?

Markos: Yes, you could put it like that. From being more self-enclosed, you spread out in spirit and find your dwelling with others with whom you are connected.

Bob: So a bit like changing houses on Earth?

Markos: Yes, rather like that, but in the different reality in which you now live.

Bob: Right, Markos. I wonder if I can ask about the surroundings or environment of where we live in spirit. After all, a house is set in a particular neighbourhood or area, isn't it?

Markos: Yes, it is on Earth and it is also in spirit. Again, it will be the surroundings to which you have an affinity, to which you feel related or attracted.

Bob: So if, for example, I would love to live near the seaside or in the countryside, rather than a city or town, would that be where I would live?

Markos: Yes it would. You would choose your own environment and setting, because that is what accords with your disposition and soul moods.

Bob: Well Markos, in some ways this all sounds very idyllic, being able to be where we wish. But do people after death also sometimes end up in places they don't like?

Markos: They can do, yes, but this is because they have built these places during their earthly lives, and after death they go to them.

Bob: Do you mean this in a sort of moral sense, Markos? So if a person has led, or tried to lead, a good life, so to speak, they end up in their chosen place, but someone who has led a thoroughly bad or sinful life goes there to that place after death? Is that how it is?

Red Cloud: May I step in here, please. What you are suggesting, my friend, does have some truth in it. As much as, yes, a person creates, has created, their dwelling place after death, his/her tepee or wigwam according to how he/she has lived. This is true. However, remember this is the start, the beginning, of the long journey home. The journey to the great spirit. There will be many more steps, many more opportunities also to move on. A person does not need to be stuck where they first arrive. As their light increases and their horizons widen, so they can change their situation and change their environment. Nothing is set in stone.

Bob: Alright, Red Cloud, but let us say for example that a person either expects to end up after death in heaven or hell, according to their belief systems. Is that, then, exactly what happens?

Red Cloud: Not necessarily so. Their beliefs may have preconditioned them for this setting or environment, but it is the life they led, what they actually did on Earth, that is more important than their mere beliefs.

Bob: So a 'good life' will lead to a different place in spirit than a 'bad life'?

Red Cloud: Yes, precisely so. As you sow, so you will reap. You yourselves determine your own fate and determine where you will find yourselves, after you have laid aside your physical bodies.

Bob: So can we then prepare for ourselves, consciously, where we want to find ourselves after death, where we will be living?

Red Cloud: Yes you can. If you plan ahead and want to consciously determine your destination, you can do so. It is left in your hands.

Bob: So is it not up to God to send us here or there after death?

Red Cloud: No, my friend. It is up to you yourselves to determine where you will go. This is the law of life.

Bob: Thank you, Red Cloud, I will stop for now.

*

Bob: Joshua, I would like to continue with the theme of, 'Where do we live?' by asking further questions. Is this alright?

Joshua: Shalom, my friend, yes, perfectly alright, we are ready to help you with this.

Bob: I have heard tell that there are 'halls of learning' in spirit worlds. Is this true and, if so, how are they constructed?

Raja: I would like to answer this question please, my friend. Yes, there are indeed such 'halls of learning' to be found in spirit. They are constructed of etheric substance, or of ether substance, that is to say of light substance. So you must imagine them, my friend, as structures, as buildings if you like, made out of living light.

Bob: So, is that sort of transparent, maybe a bit like a house of glass?

Raja: No, that is already too solid a comparison. It is much more a flowing structure of light-substance, a living building or construction, unlike anything you encounter in dense, earthly life.

Bob: Are there other buildings in spirit that are likewise constructed?

Raja: Yes, many such structures which have specific purposes, for example for healing, for education, for conferences, etc.

Bob: So do we go to such places to experience or learn particular things?

Raja: Yes you do, we do. They each have their particular qualities and characteristics.

Bob: Right, but what about ordinary dwellings, if I can say it like that. I mean houses, flats, apartments perhaps, for us to live in after we die?

Raja: 'In my Father's house are many mansions' is a saying you are already familiar with. There are many mansions, many places where people dwell, but they cannot be compared to your earthly dwelling places. They are of a quite different texture and quality. They are spiritual places, places in spirit worlds.

Bob: So are they fixed? Do they have foundations? Do they have addresses like our postcodes down here?

Raja: No, none of those, but they do have particular regions of the spirit world where they are located. People who have died will enter that region, or level, of spirit where their inclinations and dispositions, their inner soul nature, take them toward. There they will dwell, will find their resting places, so to speak. If you like, you come to where you belong in spirit.

Bob: When you say 'where you belong', is that somewhere we remain for eternity?

Raja: No, not for eternity, but for as long as that still meets your inner needs. As your inner needs change, so you will move on to a different level or region in the spirit worlds.

Bob: Right. So it remains a mobile, dynamic situation, is that right?

Raja: Yes, that is quite a good way of putting it. It is subject to change and progression.

Bob: A different question, please. Where we live in spirit do we find trees, plants, bushes, grass, stones, rocks, crystals, animals, etc.? In other words, is there a natural world as on Earth?

Raja: As on Earth, no there isn't, but nonetheless there is the beinghood of what you knew on Earth. The spiritual counterparts, you could say, of your natural surroundings.

Bob: Counterparts consisting of what?

Raja: The beings that underlie all material existence and all the different parts of the material existence. It is a realm, shall we say, of living beings that you meet rather than any external objects.

Bob: So, do we see the beings of the different trees, for example? Is that what you mean?

Raja: Yes, you see, or may see, depending on your level of inner development, the beings who bring the trees into being, into existence. Likewise with all the other things you see and meet with in the earthly world. You see behind the material appearances.

Bob: Right, I begin to get the picture, I think. So it really is a very different experience where we live in spirit, from what we know on Earth?

Raja: It is very different, but something you grow into. It is something that gradually, step by step, you learn to deal with and appreciate.

Bob: Thank you, I will stop for today.

Raja: Thank you. All blessings, Raja Lampa.

*

Bob: Joshua and everyone, the question I have today is this. On Earth, people really do live, have to live, in a vast variety of dwellings, houses, etc. They range from opulent, expensive mansions to down-and-out slums and ghettos, with everything imaginable in between.

Is there also such a qualitative range of dwellings for people in spirit when they leave their earthly life?

Joshua: Shalom, my friend, let me say this. 'There are many mansions in my Father's house' is a saying which implies that there is indeed a vast range of provision for those who come to live in spirit, and it is so. But you cannot really compare the dwelling places in spirit to those you find on Earth. It is altogether different. Spirit is not matter, matter is not spirit. They are qualitatively different in kind. Yes, it is true that behind all material things, behind all matter is spirit. But pure spirit, divorced from matter, is something quite different to what you are normally aware of. So when you ask your question, it has to be seen in this, altogether different, light.

The dwelling places in spirit are those which are constructed inwardly. You are building your dwelling place in spirit by how you live your lives on Earth. You yourselves construct your 'spirit houses', if you can put it in this way. You yourselves are both the architects and the builders of your future dwelling places, because these places reflect what lives within you. What is within you becomes your outer environment, it becomes the surroundings in which you find your home when you move to spirit. So, each person's home is an image, a creation, of their own inner life and being. Now, in a sense you could say that people on Earth also may choose, if they have the means to do so, to build a house to their own specifications and wishes. That is so. But in spirit, it is built from what lies within you and also what you have done with your lives. All this, your destiny if you like, leads you to your dwelling place in spirit. And some people will be in for a shock when they see what they have created and built for themselves. The palace that they might have had on Earth has become a hovel in spirit! On the other hand, the slum dweller on Earth may find him or herself in a very comfortable and desirable setting over here. It all depends what really is at the core of their being. Does this answer your question?

Bob: Yes, Joshua, I believe it does. But let me ask another. We not only live on Earth as single individuals; we join with others, share our lives with others, with family and friends, and perhaps with our local or even national community groups, etc. So where we live in spirit, does this also include others with us?

Joshua: Yes, it does. Through the links you have with others who are close to you, you share in the same or similar environment and setting, where you can feel in harmony with each other.

Bob: So does that mean, Joshua, that let's say a husband and wife in earthly life will share a 'spirit-house' together also?

Joshua: Not quite, but we know what you mean. Again, you can't quite compare this to earthly life because you are in a different realm, a different dimension of being. Yes, there can be, and is, a sharing, a coming together, but it is a living into each other. It is not an outer but an inner co-habitation that takes place, a coming into the others' soul-space, you can say, a merging into the being of the other. This, you could say, is a living in the same space or place. Can you understand this, my friend?

Bob: Yes, I think I can.

Joshua: Good, so this is how we live in spirit.

Commentary

From what the guides say here it is important to see our going through the gate of death as the beginning of our 'journey' into, and through, the spirit worlds. Therefore, the question of 'Where do we live?' has to be viewed within the context of a moving onwards and, hopefully, upwards into different levels or regions of the spiritual worlds. In other words, where we first find ourselves alive (as opposed to being dead) may be very different from our later experiences in these new dimensions. According to what the guides describe, it is very much our own wishes and desires that initially determine our place of residence. Perhaps this scenario corresponds to the journeying first through what Steiner calls the 'soul world', rather than the higher spirit world *per se*? It seems that we find ourselves living in the situations which somehow reflect or correspond to that which inwardly lives in our soul/spirit being.

For example, Steiner notes that:

> After passing through the gate of death, those who, because of an exaggerated sense of egoism, have avoided any form of human love on earth may be able to live only in the memory of their last earthly existence. They cannot gain any new experiences, because they do not know and cannot contact any other being. They must depend completely on themselves, because as human beings on earth we prepare a particular world for ourselves after death.
>
> (Steiner 1999b, p.45)

Steiner also points to an interesting distinction when he writes that,

> Human beings on earth are actually surrounded by earth existence and can only grasp the other world in spirit, but on entering the spiritual world this is reversed. A soul in the

> spiritual world can see our world unaided, without any effort, although from there it is the 'other world'. But to make its own world – the world where it exists after death – perceptible, the soul must always exert itself. It must construct this world for itself. Thus, when a soul is in the spiritual world, it must continually work on that world, whilst what is then 'the other world' always arises by itself.
>
> (Steiner 1999b, p.109)

So, it appears that when we pass over it is not so much a matter of RIP (Rest In Peace) but of becoming active to construct this world for ourselves. We have to bear in mind that we really do enter into quite different dimensions of being after death, to what we have been used to whilst incarnate in our ordinary daily lives. Therefore, both the guides and Steiner agree that the earthly language and terms that we use here are inadequate to describe these other-worldly conditions and states of being. It is probably also not really meaningful for the spiritual dimensions – in the same way as we can in earthly life – to separate places or locations from the living beings that we encounter. Or only so if we have actually isolated ourselves, through an egotistic, purely self-centred, life on earth.

As our journey after death proceeds, we eventually enter into, and live in, different regions of the spirit worlds. This is also what Steiner describes as going through the various planetary spheres (see Steiner 1975a). But again, how we relate to what we find within these spheres depends on how we have lived and prepared ourselves whilst living on the Earth. We either become social beings in these different spiritual regions or, because of our lack of affinity with their qualities and characteristics, become more isolated and alone. However, this situation probably belongs more to the next theme, of who we share our life with after death.

In trying to form some concept of 'Where do we live?' after we have died on Earth we should, I think, bear well in mind that, according to the guides, there is a dynamism, mobility, and interweaving in the spiritual dimensions. Therefore it is of little use to try to pin down a particular 'place' in the same geographical sense as we can certainly do whilst living on Earth. We are now in a dynamic world of beings, not of fixed things.

References

Steiner, R. (1999b) *Staying Connected – How To Continue Your Relationships with Those Who Have Died.* Anthroposophic Press

Steiner, R. (1975a) *Life between Death and Rebirth.* Anthroposophic Press

8
FAMILY, FRIENDS, PETS

What of Family, Friends And Pets?

Bob: I would like once again to connect with you and the other guides to explore spirit worlds. In particular, how we fare as human beings when we pass over there at death. Are you and the others willing to work with me again, please?

Joshua: Shalom, my friend. Yes, we are more than willing to work with you, because we realise that what you are doing can be of real benefit to many people who read what you write. So yes, let us begin.

Bob: Well Joshua, I think a pressing question for most people is, 'What of family, friends and pets?' after we die, because 'home' is really together with those we love and feel connected to. This can include our beloved pets. So can we start here today, please?

Joshua: Shalom, my friend, of course we can start here and see where we get to. Let us see, my friend, who would like to step forward first on this question.

Raja: May I step in straight away, my friend? Yes, it is a most important question which you raise here because, as you rightly say, it is the connections and links that we have made in our lives that are especially important and significant to us.

After death, my friend, you will be greeted by your loved ones in spirit after you have experienced the picture, the living picture, of your last earthly life. This picture, which is alive with images of what you have done in your life, will last for a few days and after that will fade from view. Now you are ready to begin the real journey into the spirit worlds and this is when your family and friends will come to greet you and help you to adjust to your new surroundings. Remember again that this is a process; it takes time to make the necessary adjustments to a quite new and different way of life. So this is where, and why, your loved ones step forward to help you. You are never left alone, you are always supported along your forward path.

Bob: Raja, let me try to put questions to you that I think many people would want to ask. I mean ordinary folk, with what might appear to be naive questions.

Raja: Yes, by all means do so. We will try to give the answers you seek.

Bob: Well to start with, are we going to recognise, to know those that come to help us? Won't they look very different, now that they don't wear physical bodies? How, for example, will I recognise my mother and father who died years ago?

Raja: You will recognise them, my friend, because you will immediately be drawn to who they are. You will immediately feel 'at home' in their presence, as if you were returning to see them again after an absence.

Bob: Yes, but how will they look to me?

Raja: Well, they can take on the appearances which are best suited to give you reassurance of their existence, of their living presence.

Bob: Do you mean they can appear to me as I remember them from my earthly life?

Raja: Yes, it can be like that, but not necessarily. It is more the soul-quality, the personality, you could say, which strikes you as being them. So the qualities, the good qualities, which you recognised and admired in them on Earth will be presented to you in their appearances and gestures and demeanours.

Bob: Joshua, am I getting this correctly from Raja Lampa? I don't want to colour it with my own notions or imaginings.

Joshua: Shalom, my friend. Yes, you are getting it correctly. Trust in yourself and don't doubt your ability to transmit the communications from us.

Bob: Right, thank you. So let me ask further. What about close friends, people who were important to us in life? Valued friends that we were happy to meet with? Will we meet them again after death?

Pierre: Let me step in here, please. Yes, you will. Anyone with whom you have a real link of affection and love will be connected to you in spirit worlds. Such links are not broken by death; that is, by the death and dissolution of the physical body. Such links remain for eternity, you could say.

Bob: Eternity is a very long time!

Pierre: Yes, it is, in your reckoning, but here time has a different quality and meaning.

Bob: Right. So will we recognise our friends in spirit, or rather, how will we recognise them for who they are?

Pierre: You will recognise them because you have forged that link with them – that soul link – in the course of your earthly life. Once the link is there it acts like a magnet to attract your friends back into your life and your awareness.

Bob: Are there also family and friends that we have known in other, earlier, lives on Earth, because if so it could be quite a number?

Pierre: Yes, my friend, you are right. You have made many connections in the course of your incarnations and these links endure. But remember that some that you know have been with you, again and again, in the course of your incarnations. So it is a long-term friendship that you recognise.

Bob: Well, this is on the one hand reassuring but also quite a lot to take in. Quite a revelation to meet again so many friends and family.

Pierre: Yes it can be, but it happens in stages, not all at once. Those to whom you have the latest connections will step forward first to greet you, others will follow later on.

Bob: What about our beloved pets? I mean especially cats and dogs, though maybe some people have a favourite snake or spider even!

Pierre: Well yes, people may have made all manner of links with their friends in the animal kingdom. However it is certain animals in particular, such as dogs, which have a particularly strong connection with their owners. Because of this strong connection, they have, to an extent become individualised and thereby separated themselves out from their group soul; from the overriding being of their species. Through their familiarity with their previous owners, their human brothers and sisters, they are drawn towards them again after death. So yes, it is true to say that people can often be comforted by seeing their beloved pets again after their death.

Bob: Don't you think that some people will find this a very strange picture of their 'heaven'?

Pierre: Well they might, but for others heaven is being with their beloved dog or cat!

Bob: I will see if I can ask one or two more questions before we finish this session. Let me ask something quite mundane. How do we look in spirit, do we wear clothes, do we have flowing veils, are we floating along – how do we look there?

Markos: Let me step forward for this question, please. No, you don't need to wear clothes in spirit, but you also do not strut around naked! It is much more the appearance you could see, if you were able to see your own aura in ordinary life. I mean, your own energy fields. Remember my friend, we are really energy beings, beings of pure energy. The dense physical body is a temporary dwelling for living in earth-life, but in spirit it is your energies which remain. Now, whether you want to call these energies by some names, say your astral body, mental body, buddhic body, etc., is up to you. But essentially it is the energies which surround your eternal core, as the sheaths around a flame that burns within you. You radiate your own particular light as you move through the regions, or dimensions, of the spirit worlds, and it is by your light that others know you. Similarly, you know others by their lights. So in answer to your question, my friend you – we – are beings of energy and of light, and that is your clothing in the non-material realms of being.

Bob: Do we each have our own discrete energy bodies, let us say separate and distinct from others, or is there more of a merging or flowing together? You see what I mean?

Markos: Yes, I do see what you mean. This varies. At times you may feel more self-contained, shall I say, but at other times you are more diffuse and spread out. This can vary from one moment to the next.

Bob: So what does that depend on, then?

Markos: It depends on where you are and who you are with. Sometimes you need to feel more yourself, at other times you can feel more at one with others.

Bob: So you are saying that we are not so definite or distinct or separate as when we lived on Earth?

Markos: Yes, I am saying that, but I am also saying that when, or if, you do need to feel more self-contained, then you can withdraw more into your own energy field.

Bob: Thank you, Markos, I think I will stop for now because there are new things here to think about.

Markos: All blessings.

Bob: Joshua, maybe I will resume later in the day, but for now I feel I have taken in all that I can. Is that alright?

Joshua: Shalom, my friend, perfectly alright. Move at your own pace, we are simply there to help you when you request our help. All blessings, Joshua Isaiah.

Bob: Thank you.

*

Bob: Joshua, I am keen to pick up on the theme we began yesterday, namely, 'What of family, friends and pets?' in terms of our after-death life in spirit worlds. Are you and the other guides ready to answer my questions?

Joshua: Shalom, my friend, we are, and we will do whatever we can to help you gain a better understanding of this theme.

Bob: Thank you. Now, I want to ask again quite fundamental, naive questions if you like, about how this new life is. You said yesterday, I think, that we meet with family and friends in the way that we can recognise them. But will we see them as we knew them in this earthly life, because otherwise we might just not recognise them at all? Joshua, who wants to step forward first, because I am not sure who that is yet?

Joshua: I will make a start, my friend, then others will join. So, as we explained yesterday, you have the link with the people you love after death, just as you had it during your earthly lives. It is this inner connection which lasts, which endures, not the link to outer appearances. Yes, if you need something of the outer appearance as a memory of how you knew this or that person, then the soul or spirit of that person, that being, can appear with that memory garment for your benefit. But this is not the real person, the real being, it is simply an appearance which aids your initial recognition. The person themselves, their inner spirit self, is connected to you through your karmic links and through the power of love and affection that brought you together in earthly life. Does this answer your question, my friend?

Bob: Yes it does. What about our pets though, say our special dog or cat friend. How do they appear to us?

Joshua: In exactly the same way as you remember them in earthly life, because only in this way can you recognise them. But behind this appearance is again the real being of your favourite dog, cat, or whatever. Their real soul being.

Bob: But Steiner speaks of 'group souls' of the animal species, rather than individual souls. So how is that?

Joshua: Yes, Steiner is of course quite correct in what he says, but when you have lived with a particular member of that species, perhaps for a long time, and have a close bond of love with him or her, then a certain degree of individualisation does take place. Not in the human sense of that individuation, but nonetheless that particular specialness for that animal is preserved in spirit.

Bob: Okay Joshua, so in spirit can we take our dogs for a walk in the woods, or play with our cats?

Joshua: Yes, in a sense you can, because you can create your own environments, depending on your needs and your wishes. In these wished for environments and surroundings, you can certainly take your dog friend for a walk, or stroke and fondle your cat friend.

Bob: Well Joshua, this certainly sounds pleasing, but don't you think some people would say this is far-fetched?

Joshua: Yes, they probably would, but it doesn't change the reality of what you yourselves can create.

Bob: But Joshua, if we create our own realities, then it loses all objectivity, doesn't it?

Joshua: Yes in a sense it does, but what my friend is so-called objectivity? This may exist in a world of objects, but not in a world of beings.

Bob: Are you saying that we can't really speak of an objective spirit world, that it is all subjective. Is that what you are saying?

Joshua: No, not quite. There is a common, general, spirit world, but its details are determined by the beings that dwell within it. Remember the spirit world is not solid as in your earthly reality, it is fluid and mobile and ever-changing.

Bob: But if it is ever-changing, how on earth do we find our bearings and navigate such a world?

Joshua: You do this by being guided by higher spirits, by those who have a responsibility, given by divine decree, you could say, to guide and help you through your new surroundings.

Bob: Who are these higher spirits you speak of?

Joshua: They are beings who live permanently in the higher dimensions of reality. They never incarnate into physical, material, bodies, but remain close to the source of all life and being.

Bob: Do you mean like the higher hierarchies that Steiner described in his writings?

Joshua: Yes, precisely. Higher beings of light and love whose task it is to guide and order the course of world events and bring about God's purposes.

Bob: Joshua, am I getting you right? What do you mean by guiding and ordering world events? Are we not on Earth in charge of our own destinies and determining which way the world will go?

Joshua: Yes you are, and you aren't.

Bob: That is very helpful!

Joshua: Do not misunderstand me, my friend. It is true that as human beings you have free will, but there are higher beings who oversee the world events also – who are there to help you keep on course.

Bob: To keep on course for what?

Joshua: To see that the world, your world, can evolve into what it is meant to become.

Bob: Which is?

Joshua: Which is a world of light and love, a world that is composed of spiritual substances rather than matter as you know it now.

Bob: Right Joshua, thank you. I think we are straying rather far from my original theme for this chapter. I will take a short break and then see if I have further questions.

Joshua: By all means.

*

Bob: Right Joshua, I am back. Do you think someone else wants to step forward?

Joshua: Yes, I do, here is Markos.

Bob: Markos, can I ask you some more questions about family and friends in spirit?

Markos: By all means, yes you can.

Bob: How is that in terms of ages? I mean, for example, if a child dies on Earth, does that child then grow up in spirit worlds instead, or not?

Markos: Yes, the child, the being, continues to evolve and to learn from the experiences that were gathered, even in that comparatively short earth-life. All beings evolve.

Bob: Yes, I can understand that but, for example, if a child dies, and then later the parents die, will they meet their now grown-up child in spirit? How is that?

Markos: Yes, they will, and they will recognise who that is.

Bob: How will they recognise who it is?

Markos: By having the loving link with them. It is love that endures, my friend, through all aeons or cycles of time, so to speak. Love endures, not matter.

Bob: Has this also to do with karmic bonds, karmic contracts, and so on?

Markos: Yes also that but, fundamentally, you are linked by love. If this love exists between two or more beings, then the connection endures.

Bob: Markos, what about family members, say, that we didn't get on with, or perhaps friends who became enemies. Do we meet them again?

Markos: You meet them again in order to find ways to balance out your karma. Whatever you have done, said or thought in relationship to these people will need to find its karmic adjustment and compensation. This is the universal law.

Bob: But it is different from the links of love we have with others?

Markos: Yes, it is different, a different quality and texture, but still there are things that need to be addressed and accounted for.

Bob: Do you mean as some form of punishment or retribution?

Markos: No, not at all. There is no punishment in spirit other than what you heap on yourselves. You are seeking to bring about balance and harmony within divine law. Punishment is a human concept, not a divine concept or action.

Bob: So do people have anything to fear when they die and pass into spirit? Some people fear they will be held to account, or punished perhaps.

Markos: There is no punishment, other than what you mete out to yourselves. You yourselves determine what happens to you. You create it by your own actions on Earth.

Bob: So do we create our own heaven and hell?

Markos: Yes, you could put it like that. What you have done returns to you like a boomerang.

Bob: So that could be quite a nasty surprise for some people?

Markos: It could indeed, but it is for their own higher good. It is so that they can learn from their mistakes and their misdeeds.

Bob: I think, feel, Markos that I should perhaps soon turn to the next main theme, namely, 'What do we do?' What do you think?

Markos: It is entirely up to you, my friend. You are making the choices and decisions, we are merely helping you with your enquiries. All blessings, Markos.

Bob: Thank you, Markos and Joshua, for your inputs today.

Postscript

Bob: Joshua, when I asked an old friend of mine this evening if he thought he would see his beloved and deceased dogs again when he dies, he replied that he thought not, that they would be in a different 'heaven' than he would be. What do you say to that, Joshua?

Joshua: Shalom, my friend. Well, if he really wanted to see his former dog friends then he would be able to. None of the 'heavens' or spirit worlds are separate entities, all are interlinked, so his dogs could be there to greet him if he so wishes. All blessings, Joshua.

Bob: Thank you, Joshua.

Commentary

No doubt for many people this last chapter will probably be the most important in the whole book. It seems only natural that we would have a longing to meet all those we loved and were close to us whilst we lived on Earth. Therefore the repeated questions of what they would look like in this new dimension and how we would recognise them for who they are. The answers from the guides clearly indicate that it is the soul and spiritual qualities, something of the real beings of our beloved, that are significant, rather than the outer, bodily appearances that we were once so familiar with.

Nonetheless, it seems that our deceased can take on those 'garments', so to speak, which will aid us in our initial identification of them in spirit worlds. Do we find confirmations in Steiner's teachings about our post-mortem reunion with family and friends? The simple answer to that is that we certainly do, as has already been indicated when we considered 'Who lives there?' To repeat,

> It is certainly correct to say that souls who belonged together during physical life meet again in the spiritual world and continue their lives together under the circumstances of that world.
>
> (Steiner 1994, p.137)

Steiner makes the point that after death we are connected with those souls with whom we already have a karmic connection. Thus,

> Between death and a new birth – and this begins immediately or soon after death – the dead has contact and can make links only with those human souls, whether still living on earth or in yonder world, with whom he has already been karmically connected on earth in the last or in an earlier incarnation. Other souls pass him by; they do not come within his ken.
>
> (Steiner 1995b, p.223)

We have already seen that in Steiner's accounts he distinguishes the 'soul world' from the 'spirit world', or as we might also term it, the 'astral world' with its various sub-regions, from the higher, 'devachanic world', which also has different levels. In the guides' communications about spirit worlds, these distinctions are not made. However, we can imagine that the way we relate to family and friends may vary, depending on just how far we have come in our journeys after death.

> During the first phases after death, our world consists of the relationships, the friendships we formed with our fellow human beings on earth. These friendships continue. For example, one who investigates with suprasensory

> perception finds the departed soul in the vicinity of a person on earth whom it can follow. Many people in our time live with those who have died recently or, perhaps, at some earlier period. One also sees how many come together with a number of their ancestors, to whom they were related by blood.
>
> (Steiner 1999b, p.47)

What he here describes takes place, it seems, in the earlier stages of our after-death journey. Elsewhere he says the following, which seems to indicate a later stage in our ongoing relationships with others.

> It is incorrect for theosophical books to say that man is asleep in Devachan; incorrect that he is concerned only with himself, or that relationships begun on earth are not continued there. On the contrary, a friendship truly founded on spiritual affinity continues with great intensity. The circumstances of physical life on Earth bring about real experiences there. The inwardness of friendship brings nourishment to the communion of spirits in Devachan and enriches it with new patterns; it is precisely this which feeds the soul there. Again, an elevated aesthetic enjoyment of nature is nourishment for the life of the soul in Devachan. All this is what human beings live on in Devachan. Friendships are as it were the environment with which a man surrounds himself there. Physical conditions all too often cut across these relationships on Earth. In Devachan the way in which two friends are together depends only on the intensity of their friendship. To form such relationships on Earth provides experiences for life in Devachan.
>
> (Steiner 1970, p.43)

We find in such quotations as these ample confirmation of our reunions both with more recent and also with our ancestral human connections, when we move on into our new lives after death. How that stands with our animal friends is, as far as I know, not clear from Steiner's investigations, other than affirming that animals of a particular species belong to the overriding group soul. Group souls, says Steiner, are to be found on the so-called astral plane, and the Initiate can associate with them there as one does with other people on the physical plane (see Steiner 1970, p.45). So, we do not find confirmations of reunion with our beloved individual animals in his anthroposophy. Nonetheless the guides do clearly reassure us that those close, loving bonds between ourselves and our dogs, cats, horses, etc. can also endure into the afterlife. Perhaps this is, however, more so in the early stages of our transitions to spirit?

References

Steiner, R. (1970) *At the Gates of Spiritual Science.* Rudolf Steiner Press
Steiner, R. (1994) *Theosophy.* Anthroposophic Press
Steiner, R. (1995b) *Life Beyond Death.* Rudolf Steiner Press
Steiner, R. (1999b) *Staying Connected.* Anthroposophic Press

9
WHAT WE DO THERE

What Do We Do There?

Bob: So Joshua, I am ready to resume work with you and the other guides. Just to say, the reason I am doing this work with you altogether is because I want to help people gain some understanding, some knowledge, of what spirit worlds are like. Thereby, to quote my old friend, they can feel 'more at home' when they pass over. Do you agree with my motivation and intention, Joshua?

Joshua: Shalom, my friend. We thoroughly agree with your intention and we realise that this is something of importance. Many people need to gain some clear knowledge and understanding of their further journeys in life after they have passed through the gate of death. So, well done my friend for doing this with us. Shall we proceed?

Bob: Yes, please. Well Joshua, we are gaining some picture of what spirit worlds are like, what they look like, shall I say, but what do we actually do when we get there? I mean, if I was comparing this to going to a foreign land to live, what sort of occupations could we have there, and indeed for what reasons?

Joshua: Well my friend, I think that others will be keen to step forward to provide some answers to this theme. Let us see who would like to be first.

John: I would like to come at this point. Now of course, my area of work in spirit is healing, healing in all its many aspects. Healing for those on Earth, but also for those in spirit. Yes, even when human beings have died and crossed into spirit, they have a healing process to go through. It is part of their journey here in this new land, so to speak.

Bob: John, I don't understand this. Aren't people automatically healed from all their earthly sufferings and illnesses when they pass into spirit?

John: No, not exactly. Certain ills will be healed, for example actual physical suffering and pain. They no longer have a physical body in which to register or to bring about their aches and pains. But on a soul-level there can still be much to be done.

Bob: So do you mean that some people are sick in soul?

John: Precisely, there are many forms of soul-sickness, you could say. Sickness caused by fear and anxiety, by deep traumas and hurt, by painful memories from the life just lived, etc.

Bob: So it is not going to be all honey and roses straight away?

John: Unfortunately not, but remember that everyone is well cared for. The angel is of course there, but also many helpers and friends to help in the process of healing and making whole. So, no one need worry that they will be struggling alone. No, support is there on every hand.

Bob: Nonetheless John, it still might be alarming for people to realise, or to hear, that their troubles are not over with death!

John: Well my friend, we would not describe these things as troubles but rather challenges to face up to on your forward path. After all, you are all evolving beings, as we are, in spirit. Such evolving requires learning and development and healing, in soul and spirit, to bring into effect the aims which you will set for yourselves when that time comes.

Bob: Right, John. I am wondering if we are veering off the main theme of this chapter which is, 'What do we do there?' that is, in spirit worlds. Shouldn't we be talking about what people will be doing?

John: Well we are, my friend. We are talking about the healing process they will be doing, together with the help of family and friends and the healers in spirit, such as myself.

Bob: Right, John. Can you therefore say more about this?

John: Yes, I can. You see, there is a whole team of people over here who dedicate themselves to bring about the healing process. They do everything they can to bring comfort, succour and consolation to those who arrive here frightened, scared, traumatised and feeling forlorn. Just imagine, my friend, how many human beings are dying each day on Earth under very dreadful circumstances. It is not everyone's destiny to have a pleasant death, so to speak. Some people are literally shot out of their bodies with no time or preparation for this. Such people, such spirits, need a great deal of help once they cross over into our dimension.

Bob: Yes, I can well understand that. Do you have something like hospitals? Something equivalent to what we have on Earth?

John: Yes, we do. We have sanctuaries where souls can come and rest and have time to recuperate after their earthly ordeals. If you want to call these 'spirit hospitals', then you can. The important point is that here they find those who will care for them and help them to recover from their traumas and shocks.

Bob: So John, is this sort of healing work an area to which some people who have died can also help in when they cross to spirit? Is this one of the possible occupations or jobs, so to speak?

John: Yes, my friend, it is, but it is certainly no job in any earthly sense of that word. No, far more it is a spirit vocation, a healing vocation, which those who are in harmony with this area of expertise are able to grow into.

Bob: So do we mean, for example, that if that is our inclination or impulse that we can, let's say, grow into becoming spirit doctors like yourself?

John: Precisely so, my friend. If a person wishes to dedicate themselves to helping the sick and needy, then they can grow into that role on this side of life.

Bob: That's a pretty wonderful thing isn't it?

John: Yes, my friend, you would say that because you are already a healer in your present life on Earth. So yes, for you and others like you this would be a role that you would be attracted to in spirit.

Bob: Would that apply perhaps to many dedicated doctors, surgeons, therapists, etc. on Earth when they pass over?

John: Yes it could do, but not necessarily. It all depends what sort of learning experience they need and in what direction their destiny is leading them.

Bob: So how do people find out, then, what they can or should do after their death? Do they somehow make up their own minds, make their own choices, or are they led or guided by others in what roles they take on?

John: Well, it is all those things you have said. It is a cooperative effort, a cooperative working together, to determine what is the best direction to go in.

Bob: What do you mean by 'the best direction'? Who decides what is best for someone?

John: They themselves. They can see from their higher viewpoint in spirit what lies before them. They can see what will best suit their own inclinations and wishes and desires, in order to fulfil the paths which they need to pursue to fulfil their destinies.

Bob: John, this sounds rather fatalistic doesn't it? As if they have to follow a plan that is already there for them.

John: Yes it can sound like that, my friend, but it is not really as fatalistic as you may imagine. It still incorporates free choice, free will, because this is the characteristic of human evolution. But still, the directionality, the way forward is shown to them by higher spirits who have the task to help human beings find themselves.

Bob: Find themselves? Don't they already know who they are?

John: No, not really. There are many layers, shall we say, that obscure knowledge of their own inmost selves, who they truly are as god-like beings.

Bob: God-like beings, isn't that pretty grandiose?

John: No, not really, because deep inside each human being is their essential, eternal self. That is what I refer to as their god-like being.

Bob: Right John, thank you. I would like to stop soon and pick up on the main theme of this chapter in the next session. Is that alright with you?

John: Yes, it is my friend. We are ready to work with you when you are ready. Thereby we cooperate to bring about your new book. All blessings, John.

*

Bob: Joshua I would like to resume the conversation on the theme of 'What do we do there?' Yesterday, John was speaking about healing work and the healing vocation as one important area of doing, of work, in spirit. Can I get more of an overview of what we do there, let's say in terms of tasks we might take up, rather than occupations in the earthly sense. Can we talk about this?

Joshua: Shalom, my friend, yes we can. Let's see who would like to begin today.

Red Cloud: Hau, my friend. Yes, I would like to begin today. You ask about tasks that we take up in the spirit worlds. Well my friend, there are many tasks, a wide range of activities and things to be done and I will describe some of these to you. As John told you yesterday, healing in its many forms is a very essential task in spirit, not only to give healing to those still on Earth but also to continue a healing process for those who have passed on into spirit. Healing is a process which takes time and energy, and it is essential for the total well-being of the person, the entity who lives now in spirit realms. However, my friend, you also wish to know of other important tasks.

Teaching is one of these and it is something which your guides, Joshua and Markos in particular, are engaged in. Teaching that can help those still in the body, but also teachings which assist those who live in spirit. Teaching, education shall we say, covers a very large field of activity and is conducted on all different levels.

It covers elementary as well as advanced levels of learning such as belong to the highest initiates. So, there is much to do in this particular area.

Bob: Red Cloud, I can well understand what you are saying. However on Earth, in earthly existence, we have a huge number of occupations or tasks or roles to play. I mean now in terms of what people do. They may be scientists, artists, artisans, plumbers, carpenters, builders, etc. Lots and lots of different ways of working and doing. Is there any comparison between all that and what we do in spirit, or is it entirely different?

Red Cloud: Yes, there is some comparison in that there are also a huge variety of tasks to be done and undertaken in spirit. People take up those tasks to which they have an affinity, to which they feel drawn and connected.

Bob: Can you give me examples of this?

Red Cloud: Yes, I can. For example, suppose a person was a fisherman on Earth and that was more than just a job; rather, he or she really loved this work, this form of doing. Then it is possible that on this side of life the person will seek out that area or activity in which his or her love of fishing can be further fulfilled.

Bob: Red Cloud, this sounds a bit far-fetched; after all, they are not going to go out in a boat and cast a net to catch fish, are they?

Red Cloud: No, you are of course right, my friend. They will not cast a net for fish, but for like-minded people. They will draw in towards themselves those who think and feel like them, in order to be at harmony with them. The fisherman draws in the fish as nourishment for others. The person who inclines to this activity on this side of life, draws in those who need the nourishment that comes from being in each other's company, in sharing their lives together.

Bob: Well, what you say is certainly interesting and, to some extent, I can see this. Can you give another example, please?

Red Cloud: Well, let us say a person was a builder, that his or her task was to construct beautiful buildings on Earth for others to use. When they come over to this side of life, then they will incline to find ways to construct spirit buildings, you could say, dwelling places for others to use. Their activity, their will, will be directed towards such constructive enterprises – finding ways to make their mark in the environment in which they now live.

Bob: Well again, Red Cloud, this is not quite something I had imagined, but why not?

Red Cloud: Yes, my friend, do not be limited by your own imagination, but rather try to imagine what might be the case other than you thought of!

Bob: Okay, I'll try. Just one more example please.

Red Cloud: Yes, imagine someone who was a cook. Someone who really loved preparing food for others. On this side such a person might well incline to preparing suitable nourishment for others. Not material food, of course, but rather soul-food, you could say. Food which nourishes the inner being of the other. You see, my friend, it is another form of service, a way of serving the needs of others. All tasks on this side of life are forms of service – ways to help and assist others, and these can be ways that reflect the tasks of the person when they lived on Earth, provided that this was something they really loved to do to help others.

Bob: Well, Red Cloud, lots of people do work because they just have to, not out of love!

Red Cloud: Yes, that is true, and in those cases this is not something that can be perpetuated in the spirit worlds. Only what you truly love to do can be emulated in these realms or dimensions of being.

Bob: Right, Red Cloud, thank you for now. I will stop now and resume later.

Red Cloud: Yes, that is fine. All blessings, Red Cloud.

*

Bob: So Joshua, I will resume after a break. Joshua, what Red Cloud told me came as something of a surprise. Did I receive his words aright or not?

Joshua: Shalom, my friend. Yes, you did. Keep in mind that we are trying to convey to you how it is in spirit, in words which you can understand hopefully, even though you may not expect what you receive.

Bob: Right Joshua. Can I hear more about what we do in spirit? I suppose this includes *how* we live there, having already talked about *where* we live.

Joshua: Yes, my friend, it is how you live, what you are doing there, these are the questions which you want to ask us. Let us see who wants to answer your queries.

Markos: May I step in for this. You wonder, my friend, what you may be doing when you pass to spirit. Red Cloud has tried, has given you some examples of this. Let me try also to convey something of this.

You see, your doing in spirit, whatever form it takes, will be decided by what you are wanting or needing to achieve. In a sense, everything is a learning process, and in that process you have various possibilities open to you. You may choose to do this or that because, either way, it can achieve the goals you have in mind. For one person *this* will seem the best route to take, for another a different direction will be best. It really does come down to the stage that you are at in your development and what form of service appeals to you most. Within those parameters, my friend, there are many possible choices of activities.

Bob: This sounds like how we might make choices to engage in this or that whilst in earthly life.

Markos: Yes it does, but it is transcribed into higher dimensions of being. After all my friend, you don't imagine sitting on a cloud all day and playing a harp, do you? No, rather you wish to be engaged in some constructive and creative activity in which you can play your part within the whole. Especially that you can be of service to others. There are many forms of such service and these will be offered you by higher, ministering, spirits. In that sense you will be guided and led towards that area or activity to which your talents and abilities suit you. But all will be a form of service to others.

Bob: Well Markos, I can see that, I mean, it makes sense to me what you are describing. But what about re-assessing and learning from our past life on Earth, isn't this something which occupies us after death?

Markos: Indeed, it is. You are very much engaged in reviewing your life and seeing what lessons have to be learnt from it. But this does not prevent you also engaging in some form of service to others. You can do both – both are part of your experiences in the life after your earthly death, in the life in spirit worlds.

Bob: I suppose we can only go so far with generalisations. I mean, it is when you focus on what one particular person is going through that you can get further insights. A sort of spiritual case-study, you could say.

Markos: Yes, you are right in this. We can try to give you a general overall idea of things, of life here, but yes, if you look at a particular person then you can see things in greater detail.

Bob: Well, for example, though this hasn't occurred to me before, I suppose I could ask what my mother and father have been doing since they died. Is that a valid question or not?

Markos: Well, it is a valid question, if they wish to step forward and tell you what they are doing. But this is up to them since they are linked to you through love. However, they are not guides in the same sense as we are for you.

Bob: Yes, I think I will have to think about this and see if that is something that belongs in this book or not. After all, I am working with you all in doing this, rather than with my past family.

Markos: That is correct, so see how you want to go with this, my friend. It is your choice but a choice that needs to be well considered. All blessings, Markos.

Bob: Joshua, I think I will stop for now and see what I want to ask next.

Joshua: Shalom, my friend. Good, we will wait until you are ready to continue working with us. All blessings, Joshua Isaiah.

*

Bob: Joshua, before going on to the next chapter and theme, I still want to enquire a bit further on this one. Is that alright?

Joshua: Shalom, my friend. It is perfectly alright for you to do so.

Bob: Well Joshua, I understand that teaching is a main task in spirit worlds. Is there anything like our schools or universities, any places of higher learning, for example?

Joshua: Yes there are, my friend, equivalents, you could say, of all these. There are different levels of learning, different areas of expertise, and different teachers to deliver these courses.

Bob: Doesn't this just sound too much like our education here?

Joshua: Well, my friend, it may sound too like it for you but, nonetheless, it is true that this is part of our life. Indeed, it is an important part of it because all of life is a schooling, a learning, a process of development and evolving. So is it really so surprising to you that in spirit we have, for example, institutions of higher learning?

Bob: What do you mean by institutions?

Joshua: I mean, my friend, places, locations, where the focus is on this particular work of helping souls to realise who they are on a higher level. Remember, all education, all schooling, is really about acquiring true self-knowledge. Everything depends on that. Without this knowledge, we live only in illusory worlds of our own creation. The more that true self-knowledge is gained, the more the illusions are overcome and the more the true reality of being is revealed. It is truly a process of education in the true sense of this word.

Bob: So, do you have teachers doing this at all different levels? Are some similar to our university doctors and professors, or what?

Joshua: Yes, they are. Some are standing at a high level of learning and knowledge and are in a position to be the leading teachers for those over here who enrol in this process.

Bob: Enrol? What does that entail?

Joshua: It entails being ready to make the next step on a person's forward path – the path to higher and higher degrees of light.

Bob: Of light?

Joshua: Yes, of light. Light is a substance, but it is not uniform. It has different levels of transparency and purity. Through true self-knowledge you rise into the higher levels of light and being.

Bob: Okay Joshua, this is all rather strange to me. Am I getting this right?

Joshua: Yes, you are getting it right. That it sounds strange to you is only to be expected since you are still in your earthbound body. It is not strange to those of us who live in spirit.

Bob: Right Joshua, I think I could ask many more questions about what we do in spirit, but feel that I have taken in as much as I can for now. Thank you.

Joshua: Thank you, my friend, till next time. All blessings, Joshua Isaiah.

Commentary

The question of what we actually do in spirit is another instance of those fundamental, and in a sense obvious, questions that spring to mind when we consider any afterlife. We can't really imagine being completely inactive ourselves, even if our last earthly remains may really seem as dead as the dodo!

In an interesting account of telepathic messages received by the sister of a young man called Sigwart, who died in the First World War, we can read of his life after death. Sigwart was in his early earthly life a very promising and talented musician. He died from a bullet wound on 2 June 1915 and about two months later his sister received the following communication.

> You would surely like to know something of my life here. I am living only for the great task of which I spoke before, that is, the divine music, which will be of great benefit for mankind. My work on earth was only a fraction of it. It will be something beautiful beyond measure that will penetrate all spheres and rise to the highest regions.
>
> (Wetzl 1974, p.9)

Clearly this task of his was seen as an act of altruistic service, rather than simply fulfilling any sort of personal ambition. Two days later, his sister received further information about this task.

> I want to tell you of this work. I must compose a series of difficult symphonies. One is almost completed. You would

> be amazed to hear it, for this music is different from what I composed on earth, yet the fundamental theme is the same. I have to create seven symphonies in all, then the smallest part of this great symphonic work will be completed.
>
> Others are working on it too, but mine was a special task. This was waiting for me and was the reason for my early death.
>
> (Wetzl 1974, pp.12-13)

There are several factors which play into Sigwart's special situation including the nature of the task itself, his working with others and his own apparently untimely death. Altogether, what his sister received over a period of just over five months since his passing makes for some fascinating insights. The sister says that she showed the messages to Rudolf Steiner, who affirmed their genuineness. It gives a good example of how a talent and vocation pursued in earthly life, is continued in the spirit worlds. It is especially enlightening when something of the spiritual journey of an individual person or soul has been communicated through to us. This was also the case when Frances Banks died in November 1965 and then was able to telepathically communicate with her friend Helen Greaves. The 'scripts', over two years, were then gathered together and published in the book *Testimony of Light*. She speaks, for example, of doing teaching and healing work in spirit.

> Yes, I am teaching here. I am also learning compassion, for the limited consciousness which belongs to those who did not have the opportunities afforded to me of studying the mysteries of life.
>
> Our work is to be on hand when those newly arrived entities awake to awareness. Sometimes their friends and loved ones already in these realms have been 'alerted'. Then we wait in the background until the greetings are over. In other cases ours are the first 'countenances' they see; ours are the words of comfort, assurance and welcome.
>
> Our 'patients' stay with us until they have adjusted to this new life and are ready to join their dear ones or their special Groups.
>
> (Greaves 1969, p.86)

These words certainly ring a bell with what John described as the healing work, or rather vocation, in spirit worlds. Does Steiner also tell us something about what we do, our tasks after death, in his various books and lectures? He does indeed. In the course of lectures entitled *At the Gates of Spiritual Science*, Steiner tells us in lecture five that it is deceased human beings living in spirit worlds who help to change and transform the planet, including the kingdoms of the earthly plane, and even in changing the physical, mineral, form of the solid Earth. He goes so far as to say that,

> Thus our own evolution is tied up with the changes of the whole Earth. The structure and evolution of the Earth are the work of people on higher planes, and the more highly man succeeds in developing himself, the more quickly and perfectly will the transformation of the physical Earth, and of its flora and fauna, advance. The more highly developed an individual is, the longer is the time he can spend at work in the higher regions of Devachan.
>
> (Steiner 1970, p.47)

So Steiner describes here how human beings in spirit are engaged on expansive world transformative projects, and the more so if they are already spiritually advanced souls. This important work is being overseen, he says, under the leadership and guidance of higher spirit beings.

He refers to this particular work also in his seminal book, *An Outline of Esoteric Science* when he writes,

> To physical observation, what works at transforming the Earth is the light of the Sun, changes in climate, and so on. To supersensible observation, however, the forces of people who have died are active in the rays of sunlight falling on the plants. If we observe in this way, we become aware of human souls hovering around the plants, transforming the surface of the Earth, and so on. In death, our attention is not focused only on ourselves and on preparing our own new earthly existence. No, we are also called upon to work spiritually on the outer world, just as we are called upon to work physically during life between birth and death.
>
> (Steiner, 1997, pp.99-100)

We can of course wonder what this transformative activity really consists of on Earth and why it altogether needs to take place? Since Steiner wrote about this nearly a century ago, we have become much more aware of the effects incarnate human beings are having on nature, climate and world conditions. Can discarnate souls help to counteract the destructive environmental results of our global human activities?

Although such encompassing tasks are not referred to by my guides, nonetheless the fundamental attitude of 'service' is a common theme. This attitude applies to the above descriptions by Steiner and also what my guides have told us. As Red Cloud said, 'All tasks on this side of life are forms of service.' Again, it is likely that the sort of work we can be engaged in will vary according to our own levels of spiritual maturity, as well as the particular regions of the spirit worlds that our individual journeys are taking us through between death and rebirth. So, perhaps the sort of tasks we can do in the early part of our journeys are quite different from what possibilities are open to us much later on. At any event, it seems pretty clear that we are not simply going to just 'Rest in Peace' after our physical deaths!

References

Greaves, H. (1969) *Testimony of Light.* World Fellowship Press
Steiner, R. (1970) *At the Gates of Spiritual Science.* Rudolf Steiner Press
Steiner, R. (1997) *An Outline of Esoteric Science.* Anthroposophic Press
Wetzl, J. (1974) *The Bridge over the River.* Anthroposophic Press

ADDENDUM

Climate-Changes?

Bob: Joshua, as we begin a new year and a new decade in this 21st century, the single most pressing question and concern which affects the whole world is that of climate change and what we are doing about it. The consensus feeling of very many people is that we are doing too little too late to curb the destructive, and probably disastrous, effects of global warming and climate change. So, especially in view of Rudolf Steiner's comments on the work of human beings in spirit worlds to help transform the physical Earth, I want to ask further important questions about this essential task. Will you and the guides cooperate with me on this please?

Joshua: Shalom, my friend. Of course we will. Please ask the questions which you wish to.

Bob: Right. Well, the first question must be, 'Can those who have died help us to combat the bad effects of climate change?'

Joshua: Yes, they can, provided that human beings who are living on Earth, who are presently incarnated, learn to work together with their friends in spirit. It requires a truly cooperative activity between the living and the dead, if I can express myself in those terms. You understand what I mean? Those who live on Earth now and who really want to help the whole world to move forward, need to ask for help and assistance from those in spirit. Not only those human beings who presently live there, but also higher spiritual beings who belong to the ranks of the hierarchies. If human beings, who have free will, freely cooperate with spiritual beings, then much can be achieved to bring about a healing for the whole world. But it really does depend on human beings becoming awake to the spiritual realities which stand behind the physical manifestations, and not only just focusing on the material aspects.

Bob: Yes, I can understand this Joshua, but really, concretely, how can those living in spirit, both human beings and actual spiritual beings, help us to overcome or at least mitigate the effects of climate change? How is this really possible?

Raja: Let me step in here, please. You see, my friend, everything has its purpose, nothing is really arbitrary. So, although it appears that certain things run their course according to the whims of human beings, this is not so. No, higher powers oversee the affairs of Earth. Higher powers are guiding and leading events behind the scenes of everyday happenings. These higher powers, these spiritual beings, are intent to help steer the world forward to its true, divinely ordained goals and tasks. These are God-given tasks which, nonetheless, respect human beings' free will. Yes, it may appear contradictory but, to higher vision, it is not contradictory that there is a divine purpose and guidance and, at the same time, human beings are left free to make their own decisions. So, my friend, this is why we say that it requires a new awakeness to come about so that human beings on Earth can work cooperatively with higher beings, guiding beings. In this, the souls and spirits of those who have died also partake and cooperate in the work of transformation. This is what Rudolf Steiner was referring to. The more that those of you living in the body can extend yourselves and your awareness to those beyond the threshold, the more can there come about a common – a joint – working together for the good of the whole.

Bob: Right, and how exactly can we do this?

Raja: You do this by knowing that life goes on both in this physical world and in the worlds above. They are all connected and work in harmony. It is just that this harmony can only function as it should if human beings are aware of it. They need to see what is happening on a deeper and more spiritual level of perception. If this happens, then all will work together for the good of the whole.

Bob: Yes Raja, but what should we then *do*?

Raja: You should cultivate your spiritual faculties, your spiritual abilities, in order to work in cooperation with the powers that be. In this way a beautiful and harmonious working will come about, which will benefit all of the created world and benefit all forms of life in the different natural kingdoms.

Bob: Yes, but I must still ask *how* can we do this? What is needed?

Raja: A spiritual awakening needs to take place. An awakening to the beings and forces who are working tirelessly to sustain the life of the planet and the various kingdoms of nature.

Bob: Do you mean, for example, that human beings should work together with the nature spirits and the elemental beings of earth, air, fire and water? Is that what you mean?

Pan: Let me step in here, please. Yes, if human beings would learn to work with the beings who are my subjects, my brethren, then much could be achieved to bring about a new balance in the ecology of the Earth. So many people are entirely unaware of the spiritual beings who are working to sustain the life and health of the planet. So many human beings are unaware of the being of Mother Earth herself as a divine, spirit being. If only human beings would learn to cooperate with us, then much could be achieved, would be achieved, to curb the destructive forces which have been set in motion by human beings themselves! Even now a new balance and a new harmony could come about, enabling all life-forms on planet Earth to flourish. This is possible, but it all depends on the awakening, which your guide Raja Lampa has referred to, coming about. Human beings need to wake up to the spiritual foundations of the world, then real change, sustainable change, can come about through mutual cooperation. This is what the future of the physical world depends upon. All blessings, Pan.

Bob: Thank you. With this I feel that I will soon bring this addendum to a close. Let us hope that its message will be listened to.

Pan: Let us hope so indeed.

Bob: Joshua, although I can appreciate that an awakening to the spiritual realities underlying our earthly world is important, isn't it really the physical changes, such as curbing CO_2 emissions etc., that are the most important things to enact?

Joshua: Shalom, my friend. Yes, you are quite right to point to these physical changes that need to take place, but Pan and Raja are also pointing to even more fundamental changes. Namely, a change in attitude, away from materialism and consumerism, to a truly spiritual dimensionality; to an altogether different way of perceiving and conceiving human life on Earth. This is actually a much more fundamental and radical change than even all the purely physical changes which may be undertaken.

Bob: Yes, I can see that, but without the actual physical changes we're anyway doomed, aren't we?

Joshua: No, not really. Life will go on, no matter on what level or dimension of existence that will be. Yes, even if the physical Earth falls into complete disrepair. There is more to the Earth than her physicality. And it is to that something more that Pan and Raja are pointing to. That is actually the essential being of the planet.

Bob: Yes, but what of the melting of the ice caps and the rising of sea levels, etc.? These are real, tangible, changes to the global environment.

Joshua: Yes, they are indeed, but you are not just physical beings. You are also spiritual beings. And it is by cooperation with other spiritual beings that you will be able to enact new, health-giving changes for all life forms on the Earth.

Bob: So, is this why we need to awaken to a new perception of things?

Joshua: Yes, it is. Through this, new solutions will be found to the pressing problems of world evolution and world development.

Bob: Thank you, Joshua and the others. Am I right in thinking, Joshua, that it is through the cooperation of human beings with those in spirit that we can also receive the inspirations and ideas which will help us to find such solutions?

Joshua: Shalom, my friend. Yes, that is absolutely correct. You can receive help through the ideas and inspirations which you receive from those in spirit. This is right.

Bob: So, we just need to be open for this?

Joshua: Yes, to be open for it and to realise that quite new ideas can come to you, which can open up new ways forward.

Bob: Thank you, Joshua, maybe rather like new inventions and discoveries are made?

Joshua: Yes, exactly like that. Great inventors are often inspired by those in spirit who tune in with the project they are working on.

Bob: I think Albert Einstein once said that, 'Imagination is more important than knowledge'.

Joshua: Yes, and he was right in that, in the sense that imagination opens up possibilities which an intellectual knowledge alone does not fathom.

Bob: Thank you, Joshua. I will now bring this addendum to a close, whilst the raging bushfires in Australia are now a major worldwide concern, and may yet help focus serious efforts to tackle climate change.

10
HOW LONG?

How Long Do We Stay?

Bob: Joshua, I want to turn to the theme of this chapter. Can we do this and will you or someone else start off?

Joshua: Shalom, my friend. I will begin if I may and then others can follow as need be.

Bob: Right. Well, what I am wondering is just how long do we stay in spirit worlds after our death and before we are born again, if indeed we are to reincarnate?

Joshua: Shalom, my friend. Now, this is a very interesting question you ask, because there is no one answer to it. It varies from person to person, depending on where they stand in their development and evolution. For some people the time spent in spirit will be comparatively short, for others it will be ages. It is entirely individual and therefore it is actually not possible to answer your question *per se*.

Bob: But surely there are some measures or limits or lengths of time which you can indicate for me?

Joshua: Well, my friend, you can only really do this when considering a particular individual and their particular journey. Yes, think of it as going on a journey. How long will the journey take? Well, that depends on which route you take, at what speed you travel along that route, what means of transport you adopt, whether you stop on the way for sightseeing, etc. So, it is really a variable feast, you could say.

Bob: Well, just to take one part of that journey, Rudolf Steiner tells us that the person, the soul, spends around a third of their Earth lifetime going through what he calls the kamaloca experience. He means by this, going back through the experiences of the last life from the viewpoint of those we met and related to. So, if this is true, then this gives a definite timescale, doesn't it?

Joshua: Yes it does, but only so in relation to this particular period of experiencing. After that, it really does vary from person to person.

Bob: So what are you saying? Could it be a hundred years of earth time, a thousand years, or just ten years for example?

Joshua: Yes, it could be any of those and all the years in between. It really is as varied as there are individuals to go through it. It cannot be fixed.

Bob: Right. Can you give me some sort of examples to make this clearer, please?

Joshua: Yes, I can. Imagine you have one person who has done a lot of spiritual, inner work on themselves; someone who has made it their business to really prepare for entering into spirit. Such a person may only require a very short time in the spirit worlds before they decide to reincarnate and continue with helping others on the earth-plane. They do not need long in spirit before they are ready to accept the next challenge in the earthly realm. However, another person who has not shown the slightest interest in spiritual things may need much longer to go through the processes in the spirit worlds in order to wake up, learn, and develop themselves, and to be ready to reincarnate again. It will be a much slower process in their case because they have done no work of preparation and training themselves beforehand.

Bob: So are you saying, Joshua, that how long we stay in spirit depends on our own level of spiritual development and maturation?

Joshua: Yes, very much so. The more a person has worked on themselves in a spiritual sense, the quicker they will be able to go through the levels, or spheres, of experience in spirit.

Bob: So is what you are saying a kind of general rule in regards to duration, or not?

Joshua: Yes, you could put it like that, provided you do not take it too firmly. Even within this definition, if you will, there are many variations possible.

Bob: Joshua, thank you. Do you think anyone else wishes to step forward and contribute to this theme?

Joshua: Yes, Red Cloud is stepping forward now.

Bob: Red Cloud, can you add more to this theme, of just how long we stay in spirit?

Red Cloud: Well my friend, let me try. As Joshua has told you already, things are not fixed down in black and white. It varies enormously how long a person stays here, and this is partly determined by the tasks which they take on. Remember my friend that life in spirit entails a work of service to others, it is not purely about yourself! So if a person has chosen to take on a particular task, this may mean that they stay in spirit much longer than they would need to, than if they were merely focusing on their own development and evolution. The work they are doing may entail a prolonged period in spirit worlds.

Bob: Can you illustrate this with an example?

Red Cloud: Yes, I can. Let's say that you want to help with healing, that you want to work with spirit doctors over here. Then if this is the most suitable way for you to serve, you may be engaged in this service for centuries of Earth time. Yes, literally centuries, because over here 'time' as you call it has a totally different quality. It is measured not in intervals of time, but rather in just *where* you stand in spirit. You either stand closer to a situation you are engaged in or with, or else you are further removed from it. It is spatial rather than temporal. It is where you are in relation to something else. So it is a completely different sort of experience to what you are used to in Earth life. It cannot really be compared.

Bob: But Red Cloud, Steiner has indicated for example that there may be a thousand or more years before a person reincarnates. Is that true?

Red Cloud: Yes, it can be true for one person but not for another. It is not fixed. As I say, it all depends what that person has taken on in spirit and how long, if you like, that commitment will run for.

Bob: This sounds rather like taking on a job for so many years, doesn't it?

Red Cloud: Well it can do, but you have to be careful in making such comparisons. You are in different dimensions in spirit than you were when within your body on Earth.

Bob: So does the concept of 'time' as such have any relevance at all when we are in spirit worlds?

Red Cloud: No, not really. It is not time which interests you, but the activity in which you are currently engaged.

Bob: But if you say 'currently engaged' doesn't that imply time?

Red Cloud: It appears to but, as I say, we are moving in quite different dimensions and ways of being. You cannot really compare with what you know from your limited earthly experiences.

Bob: Thank you Red Cloud, I would like to stop for now.

Red Cloud: Yes of course you can, and we can resume when you are ready. All blessings, Red Cloud.

*

Bob: Joshua, how does our stay or duration in spirit worlds relate to those whom we are linked with – either still on Earth or also in spirit? Can you answer this question, Joshua, for me please?

Joshua: Shalom, my friend. Yes, I can, at least to some extent. Your relationships with others are of course of vital importance. You are not living in spirit worlds as isolated beings but as truly social beings, interrelating and interweaving with others. You are not separated as you are in physical life, but rather interpenetrating and weaving in another. So now to come to your question, my friend. How do your relationships with those with whom you are linked, say by love and/or by karma, influence the length of your stay in spirit worlds?

Yes, since you do have these linkages, those connections, and perhaps also certain karmic ties which need to be worked upon further, for these reasons you and others will stay in spirit worlds for similar periods of time, shall we say, though bearing in mind that 'time' is not really present in the way that you know it on Earth. Far more, it is a period of being in the presence of those with whom you are connected, so that you can go through certain experiences together. Therefore, when you have gone through all the necessary experiences, when you have accomplished what is needed, then your time in spirit worlds can come to an end and you will then descend, so to speak, once more into earthly life.

Bob: Thank you, Joshua, what you say makes sense to me since, as you say, we work things out with others and not just alone.

Joshua: Yes, my friend, that is how it is. It is a working through experiences, events, happenings with others and then seeing when you are ready to resume certain tasks on Earth or to take up quite new tasks in that dimension.

Bob: Is there anything further to add about how long we remain or stay in spirit worlds?

Joshua: Shalom, my friend, I think we have covered all that is important here. Perhaps other questions will occur to you and then we can turn to those also.

Bob: Well, another question is this. Steiner describes, I think in some lectures, that in the life after death we travel through different planetary spheres in succession – a sort of orderly journey through these spheres or regions. Is that so and, if so, how long does that journey take?

Joshua: Well my friend, it is all a question of how developed and how aware the person is after death. Yes, you can say, as Steiner did, that you journey through the different spheres. That is certainly one way of putting it. What he was saying with this is that in different regions of the spirit worlds there are qualitatively different experiences to be made. It is rather like going to visit other places with different cultures and customs on Earth. Now, one person may feel drawn to this or that particular culture or way of life, whereas another will move in a different direction. So how long you would stay in a particular sphere or region in spirit really depends on your disposition of soul, your make-up and affinities. In this way it is quite individual how you actually journey and move through these regions and how long that can take. It varies from person to person.

Bob: Nevertheless it is then true that we journey through the spheres, the planetary spheres, after death?

Joshua: Yes, it is true that you do that, but *how* you do that is very much an individual matter.

Bob: Can one say in terms of Earth time how long such a journey takes?

Joshua: Not really because it is not an earthly experience but a divine experience. It is not determined by time but rather by affinity and attention to one or the other region.

Bob: Okay, but are we talking centuries, millennia, a few years or days, or what?

Joshua: Well, we are not actually talking of any of those things. Earthly time is irrelevant in these regions of spirit.

Bob: So are you saying that the duration – the spaces, intervals, call it what you will – of this journeying cannot be quantified?

Joshua: Precisely, it cannot. It runs its course according to what the person needs to experience, and goes accordingly.

Bob: Very well Joshua, clearly, I am not going to get any time-line!

Joshua: No, I'm afraid not, though we do realise that time is a very important concept within the boundaries of birth and death.

Bob: Joshua, does anyone else wish to make a contribution to this theme or not?

Markos: May I step in here please. We realise how important it seems to you to tie things down in time. But here time has no relevance in the way it does for you on Earth. Here an Earth year could be like a second, or a second here could be one hundred years in earth time. It really is quite incongruous to bring spirit into line with time – they are not compatible.

Bob: Very well, Markos, then I must accept this, but it is certainly a strange concept for me to get my head around.

Markos: Yes, we know it is, but there we are. Things are different in the higher dimensions than they are in your third dimensional existence. There are different laws at work, different parameters and different fields of activity and experience. Therefore we cannot equate the one with the other. We hope you can begin to understand this.

Bob: Well, I'm trying to. Maybe one last question, please. Do we grow older in spirit? For example, if a child dies does that child then grow up and become older in spirit worlds?

Markos: In a sense, yes. In a sense there is progression and development which you could call 'growing-up' in comparison to earthly life. However, we are not talking about the development of the body but of the being of soul and spirit. So yes, children who are beings of soul and spirit, like adults, do continue to progress in their spiritual development, their growing up, on this side of life also.

Bob: Right Markos, I think that I will stop for now, please.

Markos: Certainly, it is entirely up to you how long our sessions last; it is your choice, my friend. We simply step forward when you are ready. All blessings, Markos.

*

Whitsun, Sunday 20 May 2018

Bob: Joshua, today is Whitsun, traditionally the day on which the holy spirit, or the 'comforter', came to the disciples of Christ. This was also the spirit of truth and, I believe, brought them actual *knowledge* of the spirit. I mean not just faith or belief, but a genuine knowledge – a knowing – of spirit realities. Am I right in this?

Joshua: Shalom, my friend, yes you are. It was on this special occasion that the disciples understood, really for the first time, who it was who had been with them in Galilee.

Bob: Joshua, the whole purpose of this present book is to give knowledge of spirit worlds. Do you agree with me on this?

Joshua: Yes, my friend, we do. With you we are attempting to give knowledge to those who will read this book. Knowledge does not depend on belief, though belief may perhaps pave the way for true, genuine knowledge.

Bob: Well Joshua, I would like to obtain some further information, or knowledge shall we say, of the theme of this chapter, namely 'How long do we stay?' in spirit worlds. To an extent I may be asking you to repeat yourselves but I still want to gain deeper clarity of all this. Is this alright with you and the other guides?

Joshua: Yes, perfectly alright, my friend. Simply ask us what you wish to know.

Bob: Right. Now, one question that occurs to me is this. Does a child, say a child that has died on Earth, spend more or less time in spirit worlds than a person who has lived to a ripe old age?

Joshua: Shalom, my friend. We cannot generalise about this. It all depends on the state of development and also the destiny, the karma, of the individual. Because a child has died, seemingly prematurely, this does not mean that the child will necessarily be a longer or a shorter time in spirit worlds before choosing to return to Earth. It will have to be seen, in each case, what is the course of that individual's destiny and aims.

Bob: So Joshua, is it possible, for example, that someone may spend a very short time in spirit before making the descent to a new life on Earth? Is that possible?

Joshua: Yes, it is perfectly possible, but again it depends on what that person needs within the total plan of their life's experiences.

Bob: So how short, in Earth terms, could be the time spent in spirit worlds. Can you say this?

Joshua: Well, it could be just a matter of a few years. It could be as short as this, though this would then be the exception rather than the rule. Generally it will be a longer period of time, measured in Earth years.

Bob: Well, what would be the longest time spent in spirit, then?

Joshua: This could well be thousands of years because in spirit, time does not have the same meaning as it does for you here on Earth. For us, thousands of years can pass very quickly!

Bob: Joshua, do you think that any other guides wish to contribute this morning?

Red Cloud: May I step in here. You are asking again about how long you will live in spirit before a new birth on Earth. As we have said already, this is variable; it is not fixed. It all depends on what is needed for that person, that individual.

Bob: Yes Red Cloud, I appreciate that, but can I still ask – are there definite stages or periods of time spent in different parts or regions of the spirit worlds after our death? What I am asking really is if there is a progression through definite regions or parts of the spirit world?

Red Cloud: Yes, my friend, you can put it like this. It is not arbitrary. There is law and order so to speak, but it is tailored according to the needs of each individual. So one person may spend longer in one area, region, call it what you will, whereas another will just fly through it, so to speak.

Bob: What does that depend on?

Red Cloud: That depends on what the person, the soul, carries within itself; to what it feels akin or not akin to. It has to do with the law of attraction, but now speaking in 'soul-terms' rather than anything physical. Like attracts like, and so if a person is akin to one particular region, then this is where he will feel drawn towards. Another may not feel that same attraction at all and will rather gravitate elsewhere.

Bob: I think I have nearly asked all I can think of on this theme, so perhaps I should turn next to the question of reincarnation.

Red Cloud: This is entirely up to you, my friend. If that is where you want to begin, then we will cooperate with you on that. All blessings, Red Cloud.

Bob: Thank you, until the next session.

Postscript

Bob: Joshua, I think for the first time I have really understood why the holy spirit is referred to by Christ as 'the comforter'. Isn't it because he brings knowledge, and knowledge comforts, because it overcomes the anxiety and fear of ignorance?

Joshua: Shalom, my friend. Yes, that is correct. Knowledge overcomes fear, as you rightly say. All blessings, Joshua Isaiah.

*

Commentary

As modern human beings, our lives on Earth are very much conditioned and ordered by the passage of time. Indeed, without this awareness, albeit dependent on the accurate functioning of our watches, clocks, mobile phones, etc., we would all end up in some very chaotic situations! How often do we hear of the problems caused when our trains don't run on time. Of course, it is us adults who need to be conscious of time, much more so than little children, for whom the whole concept may be quite irrelevant. Irrelevant at least until the child wants something to happen – not later, but now, immediately!

In earlier ages, say in the historical Middle Ages, time would have meant something rather different than to us 21st century citizens. Instead of by man-made time pieces, people in the Middle Ages would have observed the passage of time through the rhythmic alternations of the sun and moon, day and night and the course of the seasons. It was a living within nature and the natural succession of events, that would have given people the framework in which to orientate their daily lives. Of course, even today the observing of how we grow-up, change and develop from childhood to youth, to adult and eventual old age, provides us with a perfectly natural chronology. Given all this that is rooted in our earthly experiences, it seems only natural to enquire just how long we are going to stay in spirit worlds after our deaths. However, as we have seen in the last chapter, the guides cannot give us any specific answers to this question, simply because 'time' is no longer a major factor for those in spirit, at least, not linear time as we understand it down here. To be able to give more specific answers to this general question would, they say, only be meaningful by considering how things stand with particular individual souls. Does Steiner's anthroposophy throw any light for us on this enigma of times after death, particularly how long before coming to a new birth on Earth?

Well, in Steiner's findings we do in fact discover some indications of times. For example, he consistently maintains that after death, when we go backwards through our earthly lives during the so-called kamaloca period, this takes about one-third of the length of our life on Earth. So, if we die aged sixty, we can expect the purification process of kamaloca to last for some twenty years. He writes,

> For supersensible knowledge, therefore, there are three corpses – the physical, the etheric, and the astral. We discard the last of these at the end of the purification period, which is about one-third as long as the time that elapses between birth and death.
>
> (Steiner 1997, p.85)

However, although this seems to be the general rule, we also read elsewhere that,

> For the human spirit, death is followed by a time in which the soul strips itself of its inclinations towards physical existence so that it can once again obey only the laws of the spirit and soul worlds and can set the spirit free. Of course this takes longer in cases where the soul has been more tightly bound to the physical. It takes little time in case of individuals who have not been very attached to physical life, longer in cases of those whose interests were totally bound up with that life and who therefore still have many desires, wishes and so on present in their souls at death.
>
> (Steiner 1994, p.113)

Therefore, as the guides say, the length of the after-death journey does vary from one person to another.

The travelling, or sojourns, in the different planetary spheres or regions of the spirit worlds also likely vary. However, although Steiner describes the successive, orderly passage through these spheres (see Steiner 1975a), he does not put any earthly times to these events. Maybe, as the guides describe, individuals will vary in their affinities for one region or another and therefore, perhaps, move faster or slower on their respective spiritual journeys? Steiner does, however, give us some timescale with regard to the total period spent between successive earthly incarnations.

> As we saw, there is an interval of about 1,000 years between death and the next incarnation, and during this period the soul is making itself ready for its journey to a new birth.
>
> (Steiner 1970, p.47)

This estimation is related to certain cosmic rhythms, as becomes clear in the following quotation:

> The length of time that elapses between death and a new birth is determined by the fact that an I usually returns to the physical, sense-perceptible world only after enough change has taken place there for it to be able to experience something new. While the I is in the domain of the spirit, its earthly dwelling is changing. In a certain respect, this change is linked to all the great changes going on in the cosmos, such as changes in the Earth's relationship to the Sun. However, these are all changes in which certain repetitions appear in connection with new conditions. For example, they are expressed outwardly in the fact that the point on the celestial sphere where the Sun rises at the beginning of spring makes a complete circle in the course of approximately 26,000 years. During this period of time, therefore, the vernal equinox moves from one celestial region to another. In the course of one-twelfth of this 26,000-year period, or approximately 2,100 years, circumstances on Earth have changed enough so that human souls will be able to experience something that is different from their preceding incarnations. But since people's experiences differ depending on whether they incarnate as women or as men, as a rule two incarnations – one male, one female – take place during a period of this length.

However he then adds that,

> These things also depend, however, on the character of the forces we take with us from earthly existence into death, so everything indicated here should only be taken as the general rule. The details can vary in many different ways.
>
> (Steiner 1997, pp.404-405)

From these last comments, Red Cloud's remarks seem very relevant when in Chapter 10 he replied,

> You are asking again about how long you will live in spirit before a new birth on Earth. As we have said already this is variable, it is not fixed. It all depends on what is needed for that person, that individual.

With this we should now move on to the next chapter and the overall theme of reincarnation.

References

Steiner, R. (1970) *At the Gates of Spiritual Science.* Rudolf Steiner Press
Steiner, R. (1975a) *Life between Death and Rebirth.* Anthroposophic Press
Steiner, R. (1994) *Theosophy.* Anthroposophic Press
Steiner, R. (1997) *An Outline of Esoteric Science.* Anthroposophic Press

11
REINCARNATION

Reincarnation?

Bob: Joshua, can I speak to you and the other guides on this theme, which I have put as a question in the sense of asking, 'Do we reincarnate and, if so, why'?

Joshua: Shalom, my friend. Yes, you can of course speak to us on this theme and we will do our best to answer your questions. All blessings.

Bob: Right Joshua, well in the first place do we reincarnate, i.e. return from spirit worlds to live again and again in physical, material bodies on Earth?

Raja: I would like to begin the conversation today. Yes, reincarnation is a fact and a necessity, unless a person has reached such a high level of spiritual development that it is no longer necessary to do so. Obviously, for the great and vast majority of people, this is far from being the case.

Bob: Well, Raja, in that case *why* is reincarnation important? Couldn't we just stay on in spirit and develop ourselves there?

Raja: No you can't, I am afraid. The laws of karma necessitate that a human being completes and fulfils his or her karmic obligations and karmic contracts in the earthly sphere. It is primarily to balance out your karma that you need to return to Earth, again and again.

Bob: Well Raja, some people may feel that is not really fair and they would much prefer to stay in spirit worlds, rather than have to go through all the trouble of being born, growing up, getting old, dying and all that. Can't we just stay in heaven, so to speak, and re-adjust or solve our karma there?

Raja: No you can't, I am afraid. It is not that simple. There are good reasons why the laws of karma can only be met by returning to Earth and meeting again those people with whom you have things to work out and resolve. You cannot simply resolve these matters in the higher dimensions of life, it just doesn't work like that.

Bob: But Raja, again some people will say, well what if we don't want to return, if we simply refuse to do so, what then?

Raja: Well, you can of course try that course of action but, unfortunately, it won't work! You will only succeed in delaying what you need to get on and do in the body. You might succeed in putting things off for a while, but not indefinitely. Karma needs to be met and healed, and for this you need to meet others on the earth-plane.

Bob: Well, let me ask a different question about reincarnation. Aren't there lots of ideas, different ideas, about reincarnation and how it works? For example, in some religions isn't it true that people believe we can reincarnate as animals or insects? Probably not plants and trees, but certainly as other sentient beings?

Raja: Yes, it is perfectly true that there are such beliefs. But we are here concerned with conveying to you facts and knowledge, rather than beliefs or dogma. The fact is that human beings belong in a particular evolutionary stream of development, and this is a different one than the animals are taking. Also, plants and minerals have their own streams, evolutionary streams, to follow.

Bob: So, are you saying that I won't reincarnate as a monkey or a dog or cat, or even a worm?

Raja: Yes, I am saying that. You will reincarnate as a human being, and you will continue your further development and progression within that stream only.

Bob: Another question, please. Didn't the Buddha advocate that we get ourselves out of the repeated 'wheel of life' of reincarnations, as soon as possible?

Raja: Yes, he did advocate that because he was so moved by all the suffering and hardship which he saw happening on Earth. He wanted to offer people, fellow human beings, the means to free themselves from these problems and troubles, and that is why he advocated they avoid reincarnation and rather progress to spiritual heights.

Bob: So, was this really a form of escapism?

Raja: Yes, you could look at it like that, but really it was born out of deep compassion and love for the human condition. It was not meant as an easy route, because in order to achieve this goal much renunciation and sacrifice was needed with regard to earthly pleasures and desires.

Bob: Raja, I am just wondering if anyone else wishes to step forward to contribute on this subject. What do you think?

Raja: Yes, I know that others would like to contribute on this important theme, and so I am happy to step back and let someone else step forward.

Bob: Thank you. Let's see who is next.

Markos: Yes, please let me step in.

Bob: Right, Markos. I am still trying to understand better why we need to reincarnate. After all, it is quite a process, isn't it, to find the right parents, environment, conditions, for the life that we need to take up?

Markos: Yes, you are quite right, it is indeed quite a process and it is not to be undertaken lightly. Much forward planning and preparation go into this process and it is only enacted when the stars are right, so to speak. That is, when the conditions are most favourable for everything to work out as it needs to, to give the maximum opportunities of actually fulfilling your karmic aims and resolves.

Bob: But surely, we can't do all that planning and preparation alone, can we?

Markos: No, you certainly can't, and that is why you are guided throughout by higher, more developed, beings who know how to bring about the right conditions for all the necessary things to come about at the right time.

Bob: But Markos, aren't there lots of things that can go wrong and disturb or disrupt the plan for a new incarnation, a new life on Earth?

Markos: Yes, once again you are right in this, my friend. However, the beings that guide you towards your next life are especially trained and especially skilled at helping to bring about the best possible circumstances. Nothing is left to chance, but all is carefully prepared and tested beforehand.

Bob: Well, Markos, this at least is reassuring to know we are helped in such a way. But still, there could be much that could go wrong, isn't there?

Markos: Well no, not really. It is better planned than you might think. Great wisdom and love goes into preparing the life-course for each person. You are never left simply to your own devices, but helped throughout.

Bob: Thank you, Markos. I think I must stop now because I am needed elsewhere. Thank you.

Markos: Thank you, my friend, until next time. All blessings, Markos.

*

Bob: Joshua, I would like to resume our considerations, or rather insights, into the theme of reincarnation. A theme which may not much appeal to many people, perhaps?

Joshua: Shalom, my friend. Yes you may be right in that. However, reincarnation is a fact of life and therefore it is important that people take it on board in their assessment of their own lives.

Bob: And how can they begin to do that?

Joshua: Well, in the first place, to simply live with this as a real possibility. To be open to the possibility that this is true, rather than some old Eastern tradition, or something that does not belong in modern life.

Bob: Yes, Joshua, that would seem a fair start, but there are really so many complex and especially tragic situations in people's lives that the idea of choosing to reincarnate will probably seem quite remote from their comprehension.

Joshua: Yes, that is of course true. Situations are complex and it is often difficult to fathom the whys or the wherefores for this or that occurrence. But, nonetheless, behind all of this there is rhyme and reason; there is a purpose to all that human beings go through. Nothing is really arbitrary or just by accident or chance.

Bob: So, are you saying that all our troubles are pre-ordained and perhaps even self-determined?

Joshua: I am saying that there is sense in all that takes place, but that sense has to be found in higher dimensions of existence and life. The problem is when everything is judged purely on the day-to-day and down-to-earth level of events.

Bob: Well yes, I can appreciate what you mean because of how I have grown used to looking at my own life, but, for many people, the whole idea of premeditated tragedies and traumas and accidents and illnesses will seem to be a total fantasy – a wild excursion of the imagination!

Joshua: Yes, indeed it may, and yet it is not. There is wisdom and guidance behind all that takes place, even the seemingly imponderable messes that people get themselves into. Nothing is without value on some level of being and experience.

Bob: Even downright crimes that are committed, or terrorist atrocities?

Joshua: Yes, even these. We do not in any sense condone such actions, but we do recognise that even these may serve the ultimate good for those involved, even though this may take a long time to show through.

Bob: Well Joshua, it is probably best to say that we can at least hope that some good will come of all the evils that are done by men, or women for that matter. Let me ask another question. How often do we reincarnate, or perhaps how long before we reincarnate after we have died?

Red Cloud: May I come in here, please? The time between lives, between incarnations, varies considerably. In some cases it can be centuries of your earthly time before a person, a soul, decides it is right to descend into earthly life again. However, for someone else it may be as little as a decade or two before the time is right for a re-entry into physical life. It is entirely individual, though of course it is also linked-up with the lives and destinies of others. You work out your karma and your karmic contracts with others, not alone. So, in that sense, there is a group karma or destiny involved in your lives on Earth. It will be up to your own higher ego, or higher self, to see what is needed, together with those exalted beings who lead you down to another incarnation.

Bob: So, how many lives might we have in total, if that question makes any sense whatsoever?

Red Cloud: Many, many lives in total, but since your evolution continues on, no fixed number can be attached to it.

Bob: Yes, but shall I say up to ten, or more than ten, or even one hundred, or one thousand, or what?

Red Cloud: As we said, you cannot put a fixed number on the lifetimes you have had and will still have. It is a moveable feast. Suffice it to say, you will have as many lifetimes as you need to attain enlightenment and absolution from the requirement of incarnating. No-one can say how long that takes for any particular person. It has to be seen and experienced, not thought-out.

Bob: Thank you, Red Cloud. Let me see. Now what about incarnating as a man or woman, or a member of this or that race or ethnic group? How is that, then?

Red Cloud: Well, you are asking quite a lot with this question, many strands to the string, shall we say. However, in short, you will choose whatever situation, of gender, race or stock, which suits your karmic requirements and needs. Fortunately, earthly life provides a wide choice of possibilities for you to survey before you make the final decision to take the plunge. And as we have said, you will be helped and guided all the way to your next earthly destination and abode.

Bob: In a way, Red Cloud, there are so many questions that can arise on this theme, that it would probably need a whole book just on this to do it any justice, don't you think?

Red Cloud: Yes, that is quite true. However, in this book you are providing the first opportunity for many people to begin to think about these things. If they look at their real questions, life questions, in the light of reincarnation and karma, then they themselves will be helped to understand matters which previously left them baffled and perplexed. So, in a sense, my friend, you and we are sowing seeds, planting the ground in which people may find the fruits which they need to enlighten themselves or, at least, to shed some new light on their questions.

Bob: Red Cloud, I will stop there for now please, and see if I have further questions next time. Thank you.

Red Cloud: Thank you, my friend. All blessings, Red Cloud and the others.

*

Bob: Joshua, I would like to have another session on this theme, is that alright?

Joshua: Shalom, my friend. Yes, it is perfectly alright with us. As we have said many times, my friend, we are ready to work with you whenever that is possible for you. All blessings, Joshua Isaiah.

Bob: Thank you, Joshua. Accepting, then, that reincarnation does take place for us as human beings, again and again, I would like to ask *how* that comes about? I mean the processes that are involved in bringing about a new, fresh incarnation. Can someone say something about this please?

Pierre: Let me begin, my friend. Yes, the processes which bring about an incarnation into a new life on Earth are indeed complex and complicated. Yet they are also smooth and well-oiled, so to speak. I mean by this that there are beings of the higher dimensions who are well used to guiding human souls to their next destination on Earth. While it is individual in each case, for each person, nonetheless the processes themselves are well known and well practised. So, provided everything goes to plan, so to speak, the person, the soul that is, will arrive in the right place at the right time.

Bob: Well Pierre, this also implies that sometimes, perhaps, things don't go according to plan. Am I right in this?

Pierre: Yes, you are right to say that sometimes other things, other forces, intervene and make the plan less easy to put into effect.

Bob: So, what sort of forces, or factors, could affect the plan, the blueprint, so to speak, for a new incarnation?

Pierre: Well, there are of course adverse forces that also work in your universe. There are beings who actively oppose the rightful course of world evolution, and these beings can sometimes also affect the course of an individual's descent into a new earthly life.

Bob: But Pierre, if this is altogether possible, should it be seen, nonetheless, as part of the person's destiny or is it really working against their destiny?

Pierre: Anything that happens, anything that takes place, will become part of the destiny situation for that person. That is what we mean when we say that nothing is left to chance, or that nothing is arbitrary. Even if other beings have managed to interfere with a person's preferred plan of destiny, nonetheless their interference will be turned to good account. The higher beings, or spirits, will not allow an intervention or interference to disrupt the incarnation processes beyond certain limits.

Bob: Well, this sounds reassuring, but that such interferences can take place at all is rather unnerving, isn't it?

Pierre: Well, it can be viewed like that but, in reality, it all fits into a bigger picture or plan which involves many individuals, many persons, not just the single one.

Bob: Well Pierre, this maybe takes us out of the norm, so perhaps it is better that you describe to me how things normally take place, leaving aside such interferences?

Pierre: Yes, that may be for the best. So, what else do you wish to know, my friend?

Bob: Well, from the earthly point of view, you could say that a new incarnation begins when the egg and the sperm meet and cell reproduction gets under way, leading to the formation of the foetus and eventually the fully-formed baby in the womb. Do you agree with this?

Pierre: Yes, I entirely agree, but what you have described there is the physical, material process, not the soul/spiritual process *per se*.

Bob: Okay, so can you say something about that process, please?

Pierre: Yes, I can. Once the individual, the soul, has decided to incarnate again, then the powers that be direct the soul to that channel, that stream of energy, into which it will harmonise. This leads to that process of impregnation and fertilisation that you referred to. Once that has happened, then the soul which intends to incarnate oversees the physical, material processes on the cellular level and brings it about that the development proceeds normally and regularly.

Bob: So, are you saying, Pierre, that the person themselves, the soul, is orchestrating the development of the embryo? Is that what you are saying?

Pierre: Yes, it is precisely that. The soul, together with higher beings, is bringing about the physical and chemical changes and developments and metamorphoses. All this is orchestrated, as you say, from above, from the spirit worlds.

Bob: So, the time factor for embryonic development, for gestation and so on, is that all regulated and overseen by the incarnating soul?

Pierre: Precisely. Everything is worked through, one step at a time, so that development takes place harmoniously and in regular order and efficacy.

Bob: Does the person, the soul, the higher self, whatever we call it, know that this is happening? Is it conscious of all this?

Pierre: In its higher aspect, yes. In its lower aspect, no. So from the spirit side of life, it is a conscious process that is enacted but this is only partly realised or known about by the soul itself. It can, and does, vary from soul to soul. This has to do with the soul's own inner, spiritual development, which has come about through previous lives and incarnations.

Bob: Is this where the idea of old and new – or young – souls comes from? Are some souls even incarnating for the first time, perhaps?

Pierre: No, not for the first time, but certainly there can be wide variations in the number of previous incarnations which have been undergone.

Bob: Right Pierre, I will soon stop, I think. Is there anything you feel is important to still add for the readers to know of?

Pierre: The most important thing that people should know is that all this is overseen by the high spiritual beings. Human beings are being guided and cared for in all manner of ways. So this should give great reassurance that you are looked after by God. God's blessing is on each soul that leaves the Father's house and begins again the descent into darkness and into materiality. The angels are forever with you and play their part in the processes which we have been talking about. This is something important to take on board and to know about. All blessings, Pierre.

Bob: Thank you Pierre, I will stop now.

*

Bob: Joshua, it is nearly two months since I last worked with you and the others regarding this theme. But because the whole concept of reincarnation, and together with it the idea of karma, seems to me so important, I want to ask some further questions. Is this okay?

Joshua: Shalom, my friend, of course it is okay. We are always ready to help when you request our aid.

Bob: Right, Joshua. Well, let me start by asking why is it important, do you think, that modern people should be open to the concept of reincarnation? Why should this matter to them?

Joshua: Shalom, my friend. It should matter because it is a concept, actually a fact, which sheds new light on many areas of life. Many things in life remain a mystery, an enigma, until one can begin to fathom it, or feel it, on the background of the possibility of earlier and later lifetimes. Through this extended picture, it is possible to view things which happen to us in an altogether different light. No longer just judging on the here and now, but allowing for the possibility that a deeper meaning, purpose and significance are attached to those things which enter into our lives.

Bob: Do you mean especially traumatic things, like accidents or illnesses? Is that what you have in mind?

Joshua: Shalom, my friend, yes, these things indeed, but also other events which might seem quite small but really do have a much bigger impact on us than we could have imagined.

Bob: Such as?

Joshua: Well, let us say you meet a complete stranger and that stranger says something to you which has a big effect on your life; something you had not imagined beforehand. When such a thing happens, takes place, it is a moment of destiny, we could say, something that was planned for as an intervention that you needed just then. However, you might only fully realise this when you look back and see what took place subsequently.

Bob: Alright Joshua, I can appreciate what you say. I have known such happenings, meetings, in my own life. But why do we need reincarnation to help us make sense of this?

Joshua: Because, my friend, seeds are sown in earlier lives which only bear fruit in later ones. Such a significant meeting could be the fruit of an earlier encounter. It could equally be the seed event for a later ripening and development. Really, the point is that nothing is just arbitrary, nothing is just a chance encounter, even though it may appear to be so.

Bob: Joshua, does anyone else want to contribute on this theme today?

Joshua: Yes, many others do. Let's see who steps forward next.

Pierre: Can I step in here, please? You see, my friend, the idea of repeated lives on Earth is not just an old Eastern concept or belief, it is also a very modern concept because it has to be viewed, or should be viewed, in the light of Christ. Christ as the Lord of Life has made a big difference to the ancient ideas on reincarnation.

Bob: Why?

Pierre: Because through his 'deeds on Golgotha' as Steiner referred to them, He has brought about very significant changes in the way that destiny, karma, and reincarnations, take place. His deeds have made all these things anew in a way, has made the inevitability of a fatalistic attitude, which very much belonged to the old concept of reincarnation, outmoded and no longer serviceable. Instead, it is necessary to appreciate that the concept of freedom and love is deeply bound up with the realities that permeate all these earlier concepts.

Bob: Can you say clearer what you mean by this, please?

Pierre: Yes, I can. I mean that through Christ's intervention in human destinies and world evolution, that the course of events is different from what it was before He lived and died on Earth. Therefore, all previous ideas to do with reincarnation, karma and destiny need to be seen in a new and fresh light. A light in which freedom, love, liberation and redemption have much to say and play. Earlier ideas were still rooted in old traditions and pre-Christian ceremonies and rituals and practices. But since Christ's intervention, all these things need to be re-envisioned, re-imagined, reborn, in new and forward-looking ways.

Bob: Can you put what you mean in simple, easy, terms for ordinary people to understand?

Pierre: Well yes, I mean simply that through Christ's love many things are now possible which formerly were seen as fixed and immovable. Through Christ, everything has new means of fulfilment, it is no longer just a one-way track.

Bob: I think I am getting the picture. It sounds to me as if destiny, karma, might be fulfilled in various ways, not just in one way as was thought of before. Is that right; is that what you are pointing to?

Pierre: Yes, that is exactly it. Through Christ joining Himself with the destiny of mankind, quite new possibilities of fulfilling karma, old karma, are now available. We are left much freer to find new ways of making amends, of healing what went wrong before. His was a healing deed which changed the whole forward course of world events.

Bob: Thank you, Pierre.

Pan, I am well aware that your voice has hardly figured in this book, probably because I have not turned specifically to the needs of Mother Earth and the natural world. I am just wondering if there is anything you wish to contribute to this theme and what has been said so far?

Pan: Yes, thank you, my friend, for inviting me to make a contribution. I would wish to say this. What Pierre has pointed to about the involvement, the commitment of Christ to the Earth's destiny, is very important for all the nature beings. It gives us all hope that in spite of man's reckless behaviours and lack of respect for the gifts of Mother Earth, that all may not be lost, even now. It is our hope that enough people will wake up to help heal the world by learning to feel responsible for the maintenance of the planet. True healing for the Earth planet can only come about if many people start to feel personally responsible for the mess that has been made in all corners of the world. It will be a mammoth job, a huge undertaking, to clean up the messes and repair the damages that mankind has caused to come about. But because the Christ is the Spirit of the Earth, it is still possible to redeem the planet from disaster. If a concerted effort is made now, not in ten years' time, but *now*, then it is still possible to turn things around for the good.

So, I thank you, my friend, for letting me come in here and make this contribution. If human beings are going to have 'a home' to reincarnate back into, then they now have to start to repair all the damage that has been done. The Earth is needed as the place where human karma can unfold and where it can be healed. So it is essential that the planet be safeguarded. All blessings, Pan.

Bob: Thank you, Pan. I will let what you have said stand as the last word of this chapter in order that its urgency be noted and, I hope, effected.

Commentary

The theme of reincarnation and karma, especially in the light of Christ's unique Deed on Earth, is central to Rudolf Steiner's anthroposophy. Much of what the guides relate to in this chapter find clear resonances and confirmations in Steiner's work. Whilst the greatest care would need to be taken to investigate any particular cases of reincarnation (see Steiner 1972a), the general principles and reasons for it given by the guides are, I think, well supported by a study of anthroposophy, as the following selected quotes will illustrate.

In his book *Theosophy*, Steiner methodically presents the conceptual case for reincarnation by due consideration of human life itself. This then leads him to conclude that,

> The course of a human life within the framework of life and death is determined in three different ways, and we are also therefore dependent on three factors that go beyond birth and death. The body is subject to the laws of *heredity*; the soul is subject to self-created destiny or, to use an ancient term, to its *karma*; and the spirit is subject to the laws of *reincarnation* or repeated earthly lives.
>
> (Steiner 1994, p.89)

In his *Outline of Esoteric Science*, Steiner states that,

> We return to Earth again and again, whenever the fruit of one physical lifetime has ripened in the land of spirits. Yet this repetition does not go on without beginning or end. At one point we left different forms of existence for ones that run their course as described here, and in future we will leave these and move on to others.
>
> (Steiner 1997, p.101)

It is in this latter book that he gives an overview of the whole process of cosmic evolution, and this includes a description of when human beings first began to reincarnate upon Earth, as well as pointing us towards future planetary conditions.

Clearly, from what the guides said, the purpose of repeated lives on the Earth is intimately linked with the concept of balancing our karma that is created in our interrelationships and actions with others. There are actually various layers or levels of karma, as Steiner specifically explains in lectures given in 1910 in Hamburg (see Steiner 1995a). The effects and consequences of actions performed in one earthly life must be encountered in the following one. This is not, as the guides point out, a means of God's punishment or retribution, but rather the all-pervasive working of divine spiritual and universal laws. It is the human being as such, the individuality which, on the basis of karmic law, sees what needs to be done in a later life to make good the deeds of an earlier incarnation.

> Thus between death and a new birth the tendency and intention is formed to make good what has been done wrong, in order to regain the state of perfection appropriate to the human being which has been compromised by the respective deed.
>
> Then we return once more to life on Earth. Our consciousness changes again. We do not recollect the time between death and rebirth, or the resolutions to make compensation. But the intention remains within us and although we do not know that we must do such and such a thing to compensate for such and such an act, yet we are impelled by the power within us to make the compensation.
>
> (Steiner 1995a, pp.13-14)

Part of what the guides described in Chapter 11 already pre-figures the theme of the following and final chapter, namely turning to the time before our next birth. Therefore, I will not discuss those very interesting communications at this point. However, the important matter of Christ's intervention in the evolution of humanity's future, and specifically in relation to karma and reincarnation, does need addressing briefly here. As Pierre noted, 'His was a healing deed which changed the whole forward course of world events.' Through the redemptive deeds of the Christ Being on Golgotha over 2,000 years ago, one major consequence was that He takes upon Himself the effects of humanity's wrong, immoral actions, for the Earth, the planet, as a whole. Whereas we can, and indeed must, deal with the consequences of our own personal karma, it is the Christ Being who alone can carry the combined effects of our misguided actions for the Earth *per se*. Therefore, Pan could say,

> But because the Christ is the Spirit of the Earth, it is still possible to redeem the planet from disaster.

Or as Steiner puts it,

> The fact that the whole Earth develops along with man is a result of the deed of Christ. All the guilt and debt that would otherwise have piled up would cast the Earth into darkness and we should have no planet for our further evolution. In our karma we can take care of ourselves, but not of humanity as a whole, and not of that which in Earth-evolution is connected with the whole evolution of humanity.
>
> (Steiner 1972b, p.51)

However, as we can see clearly today through the present endangered state of the natural world and the ecological and climatic tipping point that we have come to, it is imperative that as human beings we do all we can to now change things for the better. The Earth literally provides the ground under our feet for us to reincarnate back on to, in order to be able to continue with our spiritual development and evolution, not only as individuals but collectively as the species Homo sapiens. With this thought in mind we shall turn to the final chapter in this book.

References

Steiner, R. (1972a) *Karmic Relationships – Esoteric Studies, Vol.1*. Rudolf Steiner Press

Steiner, R. (1972b) *Christ and the Human Soul.* Rudolf Steiner Press

Steiner, R. (1994) *Theosophy.* Anthroposophic Press

Steiner, R. (1995a) *Manifestations of Karma.* Rudolf Steiner Press

Steiner, R. (1997) *An Outline of Esoteric Science.* Anthroposophic Press

12
BEFORE BIRTH

What Happens Before We Are Born?

Bob: Joshua, I would like if I may to turn now to the theme of 'What happens before we are born?', on the assumption that, having spent time in the spirit worlds after death, there comes a point when we will return to Earth, for whatever reasons. Is this correct?

Joshua: Shalom, my friend. Yes, it is correct that in the vast majority of cases human beings will return to carry on their work and further development within the confines of earthly existence, because it is also within that particular setting that they can balance out their karma and also contribute to the further evolution of the planet, of Mother Earth.

Bob: Joshua, at what point then does a person living in spirit decide, if indeed the decision is theirs, to return to Earth and to be born again? Is there a special moment for this return journey to start?

Joshua: Shalom, my friend. Yes, there is. As you know from your other reading and study, the course of life after death is not arbitrary. It follows a progression and a sequence of steps. I am now of course speaking in general terms. With each person it would be a matter of seeing exactly how this journey plays out for each one individually. However, generally speaking, a moment, a point if you like, is reached when the person, the soul, the spirit, decides that the time is right to begin the descent, so to speak, to planet Earth. The moment is what you have heard about from Steiner as the 'Cosmic Midnight Hour'. It is that mid-point between death and rebirth that is reached in the higher regions of the spirit worlds.

Bob: Is it really that person's own decision to reincarnate, or is it guided by other beings?

Joshua: It is guided by other, higher, beings. Higher that is in their own evolution and development, than the human beings in their care. These ministering spirits will guide the human beings, as souls and spirits, towards the situations on Earth that best fulfils their destiny requirements.

Bob: So the person's destiny is the determining factor, is that right?

Joshua: Shalom, my friend. Yes, that is right. In order to have the best chance, shall I say, to fulfil the aims and intentions of the coming Earth life, human beings are guided by those in spirit who can oversee the whole incarnation process.

Bob: Joshua, thank you. I am just wondering if any other guides wish to contribute to this theme; what do you think?

Joshua: Yes, several other guides are waiting to step in, and so I will step aside so that they can also contribute.

Raja: Thank you. Yes, let me take up the theme with you my friend. You ask about what happens before a new birth on Earth. Well, it is a complex process and it needs great care and planning. It is not an easy matter to bring everything about at the right time and place. This requires skilful handling of the forces and energies which the incarnation process entails.

Bob: But could this go wrong? I mean, so many children seem to be born into very adverse and deprived circumstances, that it is difficult to imagine that this was actually their choice!

Raja: Yes, you are of course right, my friend, but remember that what appears in the everyday, earthly, level of existence is not the full story. It does not show immediately what destiny is playing out and what may yet be achieved under such difficult circumstances.

Bob: Well yes, this was discussed of course in our previous book, *Trusting in Spirit – The Challenge,* when talking about karma and reincarnation.

Raja: Precisely so. Only when these universal laws are taken into account can a true picture be gained of a person's particular situation and opportunities in this lifetime. It is complex, but it is not arbitrary.

Bob: I have read that we choose our parents, our family on Earth, before we are born – that this is no accident of birth, but a well planned event. Is that correct?

Raja: It is absolutely correct. You yourselves choose the people who will nurture and support you upon Earth.

Bob: That is certainly reassuring, but again, Raja Lampa, what of those children who early on become orphans due to war, conflict or whatever conditions? Is that not a terrible state for children to find themselves in?

Raja: Yes, it is, when viewed on the purely earthly level of experience. However, terrible though it seems, even this has a higher purpose and meaning when seen from the spirit level. So yes, we understand what you are saying, but it is not all as it seems to be when viewed from a higher vantage point.

Bob: I am going to stop for now, because I need time to think what other questions I may have on this theme.

Raja: That is perfectly alright. We will cooperate with you again when you are ready, my friend. All blessings, Raja Lampa.

*

Bob: Joshua, I would like to continue with the theme of, 'What happens before we are born?' Is that alright with you and the other guides?

Joshua: Shalom, my friend, that is perfectly alright with us. Do ask your questions.

Bob: Right Joshua, let me ask this. How do we go about choosing our parents for our new birth?

Raja: I will answer this one, please. This comes about through the help of higher beings who have an overview of the destiny situation in which you are involved. These beings guide you towards your parents, and the parents are guided towards each other. In this way, the situation is best prepared to meet your destiny and theirs.

Bob: So is it correct to say that *we* choose our parents or is this choice made for us by higher beings?

Raja: The choice is made by higher beings who know what needs to come about, but the person themselves, yourself in your spirit being, is cooperating in this choice. So yes, you can say that you choose your parents to be, but the necessary help is given in making this choice in everyone's best interests.

Bob: Right. So the next question follows on from that then. Are our parents to be connected with us also from earlier Earth lives, or is it a quite new relationship that is being forged?

Raja: It can be either of those. There are no hard and fast rules in this, apart from those that link you karmically. However, that does not mean that you necessarily had a previous earthly link with your parents in this new life.

Bob: Right, but on the other hand, might there have been a long association with the same people (the new parents) that does go back into earlier incarnations?

Raja: Yes, it could be so, but again, not necessarily so. It really does come down to the particular situation, the karmic situation, in which you place yourself.

Bob: What about the actual place of the birth, our birth, in terms of the country, nationality, local environment, etc. Is that also chosen somehow by us?

Raja: Yes, it is of course, through the choice of your parents-to-be. The one follows on from the other. But it is the human connections which come first, and then the geography follows thereafter.

Bob: Another question. Do we know, before we are born, what we want to achieve with the coming lifetime?

Raja: Certainly you do. That is the whole point of it. You have set karmic goals and aims, in spirit, which need to be enacted in the life on Earth.

Bob: But why then do we not remember these aims and goals when we are incarnated?

Raja: To some extent you do, but the degree to which you become conscious of your aims varies from person to person. Some people know from an early age what they want to do and become. Others flounder around, trying to make sense of their life's course. So there are all manner of variations on this theme.

Bob: Can things actually go wrong then? I mean in the sense that the goals and aims are simply not achieved at all?

Raja: Yes, such things are possible, but usually not so. Usually, at least to some extent, the aims and goals are fulfilled and the plan is enacted as it was prepared beforehand.

Bob: But if that does not happen, why not?

Pierre: Let me come in here, please. If things do not go according to plan then there is a breakdown, a disconnect, between the higher self and the lower, earthly self. For whatever reason the person is then estranged from themselves, and this is a form of soul illness. Because of this, the life can become chaotic and the karmic aims cannot be fulfilled in this lifetime. In such extreme cases, another life will be needed to pick up the pieces and try again to do what was not possible in that last life.

Bob: But Pierre, cannot the angels or other higher beings sort out the problems – heal the disconnect?

Pierre: No, this cannot be done just like that. It is a complex process and it requires an intervention which still has to respect human free will. However, we are here talking about unusual cases, rare cases, not the normal course of events.

Bob: Well perhaps then we should rather keep to what more usually takes place. Another question. I've read in Steiner's works that there is a 'pre-vision' of the life to come, perhaps similar to the vision after death of the life we had. Is this true, and if so, why do we have it?

Pierre: Yes, it is true and people, or rather souls, have it in order to be prepared for what is to come. Forewarned, forearmed, you could say.

Bob: Okay, but Steiner also says that in some cases, for some souls, the prospect of the coming life is too much for the soul to bear, and then the soul can turn back to spirit and withdraw. Is that also true?

Pierre: Yes, it is true that this can happen, but not so in the great majority of cases. But yes, it is always a possibility.

Bob: And if the soul does then withdraw, what does that mean for the child's life, for example?

Pierre: It could mean a number of things. Premature illness or even death could follow, or psychological problems in coming to terms with the growing up process.

Bob: But would this actually be part of the karmic situation which the person chose after all?

Pierre: No, not really by choice, but rather by fear and rejection of what the coming life held in store. So it does get really complicated, but nonetheless there will be karmic compensations, as well as karmic consequences, in these particular situations.

Bob: Well Pierre, I realise we are talking about exceptions rather than the rule. So, if all does go well, according to plan that is, then the way to Earth is smooth, so to speak?

Pierre: Yes, it is, and this is the case for most people, even if they are then born into very testing times.

Bob: What sort of consciousness do we have, then, when we leave spirit and come into Earth-life anew?

Pierre: Well, the consciousness changes from having a much more expanded, universal consciousness, to gradually becoming narrower and narrower. This is a process, of course, and does not happen from one moment to the next. Nonetheless, eventually the person acquires their pointwise ego-consciousness as an earthly human being.

Bob: Is it joyful or painful to come into incarnation again?

Pierre: It is both. It is a joy to be able to take up a body in order to fulfil the chosen destiny, but it is also a pain to be restricted in a body of flesh and blood compared to the lightness of spirit existence.

Bob: So, it is a sort of two-edged sword?

Pierre: It is indeed. A two-edged sword, which is the lot of all human beings who are, actually, spirit beings first and foremost.

Bob: Pierre, is there anything else that is important for readers to know on this theme please?

Pierre: Well there are many aspects of all this – it is really a very complex process – but we feel that you have covered the main points of interest with your questions. We would only add that it does require great courage and determination to go back into a physical body and to take up the tasks which await you in your earthly lives. So, well done for that, my friends. We salute you for that. All blessings, Pierre and the others.

Bob: Actually Pierre, one further question. How is it with our guardian angel? Does the angel accompany us through the incarnating process?

Philip: So, this is clearly a question for me. Yes, each person's guardian angel will be with them throughout this process, just as this has been for the person in all their other births, deaths and lives. The angel provides the connecting link with the person's true spirit self.

Bob: So, to know this must be very reassuring, don't you think?

Philip: Yes, it should be, but this all depends how conscious the person is of their angel. In this respect, much needs to be done to awaken this awareness more generally.

Bob: Well, I hope this book will help with this.

Philip: Yes so do we. All guardian angels would wish to have a conscious relationship with their human charges.

Bob: So, thank you, Philip, for this.

Philip: Thank you, my friend and brother. All blessings, Philip.

Bob: Joshua, still one more question please. What about any brothers and sisters in our family? Presumably they have also chosen to be with those parents, as we have. So, how is that with all of us in the same family group?

Joshua: Shalom, my friend. Yes, this is an important question because it points to the group-soul situation within the family. You and they, all of those in the family, have a group karma to carry as well as an individual karma. You all come together to work out and balance your destinies, your karma, together. So this is again nothing arbitrary, it is a choice made in spirit to bring you all together in one place, so to speak. It then gives the opportunities you all need to sort out your karma together and do what is needed.

Bob: But Joshua, sometimes families, siblings, can have a lot of conflict and difficulties between them.

Joshua: Yes, they can, and this is precisely why they should take every opportunity to sort things out for the best. Old karma, past deeds, need to be addressed and made good by all that can be done to restore harmony in the current lifetime.

Bob: Except it doesn't always work, sometimes difficulties are exacerbated!

Joshua: Yes, sometimes they are, but whatever is not dealt with now will have to be dealt with at a later time and in a subsequent incarnation. Karma and its laws need to be met and fulfilled. There is no getting away from that.

Bob: Well, fortunately Joshua, sometimes siblings also get on really well and support each other.

Joshua: Yes, and that is all to the good!

Bob: Thank you, Joshua, that was really the question I still needed to ask.

Joshua: Shalom, my friend. All blessings, Joshua Isaiah.

Commentary

This chapter should help give us much reassurance that our earthly birth is neither arbitrary nor fatalistic, but rather a lovingly planned event which we have ourselves orchestrated from spirit, together with higher beings. We know of course that the situations and circumstances surrounding human beings' births vary enormously, and sometimes great difficulties are encountered right from the start. However, the guides tell us that much preparation has taken place, well in advance, in order that the incarnating soul can have the best opportunities for fulfilling his or her destiny, or karma, in the life to come. They tell us also that after the journey through spirit worlds, following our previous death, there comes a point where we resolve to descend once again to the earth-plane. This point, midway in our afterlife journey, is called by Steiner the 'Cosmic Midnight hour'. He says,

> As we thus live on further during the first half of life between death and a new birth and approach the middle of this period, we feel the inner life of solitude growing richer and richer, while the times of vision of the spiritual environment become shorter and dimmer. This continues until the middle of the period between death and a new birth, the time which in my last Mystery Play *The Soul's Awakening,* I have described as the Cosmic Midnight. This is the time when the inner life of the human being is at the point of greatest intensity, but he has no longer within him the creative soul-force to illumine his spiritual

> environment... And now begins the time when there develops within us the longing for creative power; for although we have an infinitude as our inner life, the longing awakens within us for an outer world once more.
>
> (Steiner 1959, pp.91-92)

This longing leads us, stage by stage, in our descent through the spirit worlds towards our new birth on Earth. In this process, as the guides say, we are guided and helped by ministering spirits. The individual on the way to reincarnation needs to again acquire the 'garments' in which the spirit is clothed, so to speak. That is a new astral or soul-body, and a new etheric or life-body. The new physical body *per se*, will be provided by the parents-to-be. In an early course of lectures by Steiner we find that,

> For the next stage, help is needed. Higher Beings, the Lipikas, guide the germinal human being to the chosen parents; the 'Maharajas' form the etheric body to correspond with the astral form and with the contribution by the parents to the physical body.

A little later in the same lecture he says,

> Parents who will be exactly right for the germinal human being cannot always be found; all that can be done is to search for the most suitable. Similarly, a physical body cannot always be built so as to match exactly the incoming etheric body. There can never be complete harmony. This is the reason for the discord between soul and body in human beings.[2]
>
> (Steiner 1970, p.49)

That things do not always, if at all, work out perfectly in terms of our incarnating back into earthly life is perhaps understandable, given the high numbers of children being born each day on the planet. Though many of us would like a perfect life, in reality we have to get on and do

[2] The rather Indian sounding names for higher beings in this quote reflect the terminology prevalent in the Theosophical Society circles which Steiner spoke to before founding his own Anthroposophical Society in 1913.

our very best with the cards we are dealt. That being said, whilst hopefully the great majority of children will feel well-received into loving families, there will be some who, even with that benefit, don't seem to fit well into life on Earth and experience difficulties and estrangement (see Hogenboom & Woodward, 2013). However, whatever circumstances do befall us in life, we can, I believe, be assured that all earthly experiences will be turned to good use in the greater spiritual scheme of karmic balancing and compensations. In other words, nothing is for nothing, and nothing will go to waste. Eventually, all our life's experiences will be taken with us, after death, as the hard-won fruits of this current incarnation. Finally, as Pierre pointed out to us in Chapter 12,

> We would only add that it does require great courage and determination to go back into a physical body and to take up the tasks which await you in your earthly lives. So, well done for that, my friends. We salute you for that.

References

Steiner, R. (1959) *The Inner Nature of Man – And the Life Between Death and a New Birth.* Anthroposophical Publishing Company

Steiner, R. (1970) *At the Gates of Spiritual Science.* Rudolf Steiner Press

Hogenboom, M, & Woodward, B. (2013) *Autism – A Holistic Approach.* Floris Books

APPENDIX: CONVERSATIONS WITH MY FATHER IN THE AFTERLIFE

The idea to include this Appendix came about as follows. In December 2019 I received feedback on the MS from a friend who, like myself, is a serious student of Rudolf Steiner's anthroposophy. He pointed out that Steiner had focused on 'concrete destinies' of individuals, in addition to his more general writings about the higher worlds. In particular, my friend referred to specific lecture courses that Steiner gave in 1924, in the year before his terminal illness in 1925. This friend also remarked that personally he would be '... more interested in questions that really live in you, and go beyond what we already know from one hundred years ago.' What he was pointing to with these comments was immediately clear to me, and was indeed the reason why I have decided to include this Appendix.

Interestingly, when referring to Rudolf Steiner's more general descriptions of the journey which we undergo between death and a new birth on Earth in my *Introduction* to this book, I noted that usually these lacked specific, individualised, scenarios. I wrote that,

> To obtain the latter, it would probably be necessary to follow a particular soul on their unique pathway after death.

My friend's comments reminded me of this, and this in turn led me to the following thought. Namely, that I could, perhaps, try to come into telepathic communication with my father, who passed into spirit nearly 25 years ago. If he was indeed willing to cooperate with me in this dialogue, I could ask him to describe something of his own journey into the higher worlds. Naturally I would only include such information in this Appendix for others to read if my father was happy to agree to this. So this was the proposition which came to my mind. This would then constitute a unique, personal and 'concrete destiny' to augment the contents of this book as provided by my spirit guides. However, before I continue, I would like to include the following background information.

My father, Sidney Ronald Woodward, known to friends and family as 'Ron' or 'Ronnie', was born on 4 August 1911 and died on 18 January

1995, aged 83. He passed over whilst in our small local hospital, where he had been admitted shortly after Christmas 1994 due to his deteriorating physical health. This was because of repeated strokes, which had first begun in early September of that year. Unfortunately, these strokes had increasingly affected my father's abilities to walk, maintain balance, to speak and write. For someone who, until then, had led an active life, in spite of his chronic angina condition, these disabilities were a severe blow. In his working life he had been both a company secretary and an accountant, and in both these roles he had shown a high ethical and professional standard. When he took early retirement in his sixties, my father discovered latent talents as a keen amateur artist working in oils, and a poet. This gave much pleasure both to himself and others. However, he was also a genuine seeker after truth and, in later life, he became a member of the Anthroposophical Society in Great Britain. I well remember how he read with great interest the basic books of Steiner which I regularly presented him with. He was particularly taken with the lectures which Rudolf Steiner gave to the workers at the Goetheanum building. This was located at Dornach in Switzerland and was intended to be the physical centre of the worldwide General Anthroposophical Society.

Certainly, through our common interest in anthroposophy, my father and I shared an active spiritual link, in addition to that familial love which unites a father to his son and vice versa. So, with these words I think I have said enough. My next task will be to sit down at an appropriate time to see if I can converse with 'Ron', and enquire about his own post-mortem life.

Conversations

This and the following conversations took place directly after my usual daily morning meditations.

To initiate this process I have sat myself down to quietly remember, with love, gratitude and respect, my father. Before me are set out several photographs, showing his appearance at different ages and stages of life. As I have pointed out previously, it is essential in all spiritual work to approach this activity in the right mood of heart and mind.

13th December 2019:

Bob: Father, are you able and willing to come into communication with me, for the purpose of sharing something of your experiences in spirit over the past 25 years? You must feel no coercion, obligation,

or imposition over this question. It should be, must be, something which you can do in love and freedom.
[I experienced then an immediate response, in the same way as when working with my guides.]

Ron: My son, I am more than happy to speak with you and to do my best to tell you of my experiences and life over here. I have waited for a long time to be able to do this, because it was up to you to ask me, rather than for me to impose myself upon you. So, Robert, I thank you for this and I will respond to your request with the greatest pleasure. All my blessings, Dad.

Bob: Thank you, father. This was all that I wanted to be clear about today. I will initiate a proper conversation with you when I next sit down for this specific purpose. My love and thanks to you.

*

14th December 2019:

Bob: Father, I would like now to hear of some of your experiences since you entered into spirit, following your earthly death in January 1995. I would like to leave you quite free to tell me whatever you wish to. Perhaps later I may wish to ask you specific questions but, for now, I want to leave it entirely up to you what you wish to share with me. Is that alright with you?

Ron: Robert my son, it is perfectly alright with me. I will do as you suggest and simply try to tell you of my journey so far. All blessings, Dad.

Bob: Right then, over to you please.

Ron: My son, let me first say what a blessing it was that you were able to care for Joan [my mother] after my passing on, the way that you did. I was well aware from spirit how you cared for her, and of the bond of love which existed between you both. For this I am eternally grateful. Thank you, my son.
Now, how was my own journey into this new life after my death? Well, to begin with it was exactly as I had been led to understand through my study of Steiner's writings. I saw my whole life spread out before me and I was able to take it in, in its entirety. This is a truly remarkable experience, because without any effort at remembering, it is simply there to behold. Although I had heard descriptions of this before I died, when it happened it was a wonder to behold – the whole of life spread out before me. So this was the first mighty, panoramic, experience I had after death. However, together with this

was my awareness of my family and friends from my previous, former, life on Earth, coming to greet me and welcome me into this new form of existence. It was such a joy to meet again my dear mother and father whom I had not seen for so many Earth years. Especially my mother, Bessie, who had died when I was still quite a young man. [She died in 1936, when father was 25.] Oh what a joy to see her again and looking so well and full of life. You can hardly imagine, Robert, what a blessing it is to meet again those souls, those people, who have been instrumental in one's own life on Earth. It is truly a coming together, a reunion, after many years of separation. So this, my son, is something which it is very important for others to know of. Death is not the end, but it is the beginning of a new and rich and joyful life in spirit worlds.

Yes, this reunion lasts then actually for a long time, but it cannot be compared to earthly time. Rather it is a coming together, a being at one with those whom we loved on Earth. It is the love which unites us and enables us to find each other in the land of light and love, for that is truly what it is. A land where all those whom we love are to be found again, well and whole in their being. This much I wanted to say first because I realise that for many, many people living on Earth there is really no idea of what to expect after death. There are so many wrong ideas, misguided ideas about what life will be like, or even no belief at all that there will be any life after we die. This is quite wrong; there is life in abundance. Life here flows like running water on Earth. As rivers, streams and even the oceans and seas flow and ebb, to and fro, forwards and backwards on Earth, so in the land of spirits, life itself is a flowing substance, a reality that is apparent to all who are no longer trapped inside the illusion of the material world.

I will tell you more of my experiences and I am grateful that you are not imposing your thoughts on mine, because otherwise it would be more difficult for me to express what lives in me, to you. So, Robert, life continues here in ways which those on Earth, including of course myself when I lived there with you, have no idea about. There is a richness, an intimacy, a living in the other, which is unknown in earthly life, except at rare moments when a person may feel totally united with another person. In truth, such moments are rare on Earth, precisely because the physical body gets in the way of this. Over here, things are totally different. There are no barriers to complete union with another person or being, other than those which we construct for ourselves. We can make barriers, we can enforce our own limitations if we have that soul-set to do so. But this is very much up to us. We can lock ourselves up in a box, so to speak, if we choose to do so, but if we do, then we exclude ourselves from truly experiencing the freedom and blessing of these worlds, and of God's grace. Yes, it is indeed God's grace, the grace of the being that lives in 'all that is', that really drives forward the whole course of world events, both in the earthly and the spiritual worlds. However, of course, human beings as you know have freedom of will, at least to an extent, and therefore they can at any moment isolate themselves from the reality, the greater reality, which is there to behold and to be part of. None of us are really isolated beings, but it can appear so, because of the boxes into which we put ourselves. Yes, we do it to ourselves, it is not done to us. So again, my son, it is important that people realise how these situations of life and existence after death can be constructed through their own mindsets and beliefs. This is something which I have learnt more and more, in the time that I have been here.

I realise, my son, that you are feeling a little tired with bringing through my words and thoughts. If you need a break, then take it. We will be able to pick up the thread at any time, now that the door has been opened through your initiative.

Bob: Yes father, I think I will indeed bring this session to a close and go out and have a walk on this sunny morning with blue skies. So, until next time, my thanks to you, father.

(*This session lasted about 40 minutes.*)

*

15th December 2019:

Bob: Father are you willing to tell me more of your experiences and your journey in spirit?

Ron: Robert, my son, I am more than willing to do just this, because I also realise the aim which you have in writing this Appendix as part of your new book; namely, to help others to understand something of the nature of the Afterlife into which they will also pass when they meet their earthly deaths. So yes, I am happy to be able to help you and others in this respect.

Bob: Thank you, father. Although I do have real questions which I would like to ask you, I will keep those for later. Now I ask you to simply share with us whatever you can of your own, personal experiences, please. I leave it entirely up to you how you do this.

Ron: Thank you. Let me begin by saying the following. I was amazed by what I experienced after my passing in the hospital. As you know, Robert, my illness had robbed me of my power of speech, and this to me was a great blow. It was very hard not to be able to communicate with you, Joan and others who were caring for me. Yes, I tried through my expressions to convey what I was feeling and thinking but, without speech, this was difficult if not impossible. So you can imagine my relief when, free of the body, I found that I could again speak, communicate, to those around me. Yes, not with human words, in the sense that we use these in daily life on Earth, but rather directly through thoughts. Actually, in the same way as we are doing now. I discovered that I could communicate at will with those who came into my orbit of consciousness. These included, of course, my close family and friends who had preceded me into the afterlife. What a joy it was, Robert, to be able to speak again with my own dear mother and father, and then also with my sisters with whom, as you know, things had not been plain sailing during the last years of life. Now, however, I could put aside those difficulties, and meet those souls afresh. Can you imagine, Robert, how relieved I was to find myself with those with whom I had bonds of love? Well, I can only tell you that this seems to be the common lot of those who pass on after death. That they are again united, reunited, with those whom they loved in life on Earth. This is something of great joy which I feel everyone should know about, and this is why I wanted first to tell you this today.

Now I will go on to tell you other things about my life in spirit. For a start, it is not what you might imagine, or conjecture, when living on Earth in a body of flesh and blood. It is a mistake to imagine this life, this world, as comparable to what you normally have around you in daily life. No, it is raised into a different dimension altogether. Light in different qualities, shades, colours, intensities, is an all-pervading feature of this world. Yes, you do, of course, have light in different intensities also in the earthly world, but it cannot really be compared to the flowing quality of the light over here. This is of a different dimensionality. In the light, live beings. It is a world of beings, not of things, as your guides have already told you. It is, then, a matter of getting to know the beings that dwell within these realms of light. These include human beings, human souls, we can say, but also beings of a different order; beings who never need to incarnate into earthly bodies. These beings are angels and other higher beings. We can see that they are 'higher' by the intensity of the light which they radiate. Gradually we get to know beings on all different levels who, nonetheless, share in this one world. I say one world, even though it has many differentiations and parts. But the parts constitute a wholeness. Yes, 'in my Father's house are many mansions', but all these mansions belong together and form a wholeness, a one-ness. This may be difficult for you to conceive, Robert, but nonetheless this is the truth of the matter, and it is about the truth that I speak to you.

Now, let me say more about the journey, the journeying in these higher dimensions of experience and being. When we move from one level to another, it is that we experience a lightening of our being, of our soul and spirit. We feel as if we are given wings, if I can express myself in this way. As if we are given the means to fly higher, into higher regions of the spirit. This is what it feels like. And in this process, this elevation, you could say, we are allowed to meet the beings of higher worlds. Beings who are closer to God – to the Creator being of the universe. It is with a feeling of deep reverence and devotion that we are allowed, permitted, to rise into these heights of the spirit world. And when we come into these regions, we realise that we come closer to the creative forces of the cosmos. That is to say, to the beings who weave the very fabric of the universe which you see with your physical eyes, and which you can marvel at when you extend your gaze outwards. This is what we are allowed to see for ourselves when we rise into the higher regions of existence. It is truly a sight to behold, and makes one feel very humbled to be allowed into this workshop of the gods, if I may put it like this. When we come to these regions, we are also made aware of how our own destinies are forged, not now by the higher gods, but actually by we ourselves. We become aware that we are the architects, the shapers, of our own lives. Yes, even of our multiple earthly lives. For, as you know from your studies Robert, we live not once but many lives on planet Earth. And these lives have been fashioned by us through the higher wisdom which we gain during our times in the afterlife because here, in the spirit, we can gain an overview, a wide perspective, of what we need to do in order to make our own unique contribution to the course of world events. We feel a responsibility, a deep responsibility, to play our part in the plan of creation, in the plan of world evolution towards love and light, and peace and harmony.

All these things I have learnt to recognise, to know, since I have lived in spirit worlds over the last quarter of a century; that is, measured in Earth-time. This much I wished to share with you this morning. All blessings, Dad.

Bob: Thank you. Joshua, was I really bringing through accurately what my father wanted to say?

Joshua: Shalom, my friend. Yes, you were. We realise that all this may seem to require you to expand your horizons of credibility, but yes, you were bringing through what he gave to you. All blessings, Joshua Isaiah.

(*This session lasted about 45 minutes.*)

*

16th December 2019:

Bob: So father, I wish to link up with you once again this morning and ask you questions – questions which I have, and which you may be able to answer for me. Are you willing to do this?

Ron: Yes Robert, I am more than willing to be of whatever help I can to you. So, please ask your questions and I will answer them to the best of my ability.

Bob: Right. Are you happy living in spirit?

Ron: Yes, I am very happy here. It is a very different environment from when I lived in my earthly body. It is a place of lightness, of light and love, and a place where we can work on ourselves and on the world from a higher vantage point. So yes, in answer to your question, I am happy in my present surroundings and situation.

Bob: Are you together with mother in this place, somehow?

Ron: Yes, I am. Your mother and I as kindred souls have a belonging together in this place, linked by love and the feeling of togetherness which we also had in our Earth lives as husband and wife.

Bob: But, presumably, in spirit you are no longer husband and wife?

Ron: That is correct. Here we are souls that are linked by our love for each other, but not bound by any earthly laws or ties.

Bob: This kinship which you know in spirit, is this something which others have also? Is this a way of being which many who pass over can look forward to?

Ron: It is indeed. It is the norm, so to speak, that those who had loving ties on Earth will continue to have these ties also after death. It is our love that links us together.

Bob: But how is it if we have made enemies in our Earth lives, have really had great antagonism to certain people?

Ron: Well, in that case you have something important to do with just those people, those souls, after death. You will seek to make recompense for the ill-feelings you had on Earth for that particular person and to find ways to heal that rift and disharmony.

Bob: Where do you now live?

Ron: I live in a region of the spirit worlds where I can work productively. I mean by this, where I can join with others to help the progress of the world; the world where you live out your earthly life.

Bob: Can you see us on Earth? For example, can you see me now at your old bureau, sitting down and writing out these communications?

Ron: Yes, I can. Because you are linking up with me I can perceive you from this side of life and see what you are doing.

Bob: Right, but do you perceive me physically, or is it some other kind of percept you have?

Ron: I perceive you in your energy being, if I can put it like that. I perceive the energies and currents of force, of life, that are within and around you as you actively communicate with me.

Bob: So is this like looking at the auric field, the human aura, my aura. Is this what you see?

Ron: Yes, it is. I see you as extended outwards and as occupying a space which is larger than your physical, material body.

Bob: Can those in spirit, like yourself, father, perceive what is going on on Earth, within the Earth sphere?

Ron: Yes, we can, and we take great interest in all that is happening in the earthly world. It is something which occupies us very much, because we know that we ourselves will be returning to that plane of action.

Bob: Can those in spirit help human beings on Earth; can you assist us in our lives?

Ron: Yes, again, we can, but only when we are called upon to do so. We cannot interfere in your free will.

Bob: But for example, if I am concerned, let's say, with what's going on within the family and want to help with this, can you also help?

Ron: Yes I can, if you ask me to, but not otherwise. It is the asking which gives us on this side permission to intervene as best we can.

Bob: And what sort of interventions are possible for you?

Ron: Only those which do not interfere with your own choices and decisions. We can only send helpful, positive influences to help change very negative energies or expressions.

Bob: Is that easy to do?

Ron: Not always. It all depends how open the person is to receive assistance and help. If the openness is not there, then there is little we can do.

Bob: Can you describe something of your present environment? Are there features, things, which give it a certain appearance?

Ron: No, there aren't. You cannot compare it to what you know on Earth. It is of an altogether different quality of being. We are in a world or land of beings, not of things. It is the qualities of different beings, of souls and spirits, that constitute our environment here.

Bob: Yes, but is there anything of music, sound, colours, textures, etc. that bear some resemblance to earthly life?

Ron: No, not to earthly life, but yes to heavenly life! Yes, there is music – the harmony of the spheres, the angelic choirs, the music of the oceans of life. And yes, there are colours, energies and tones of various kinds. But these are the manifestations, the expressions, of living beings. Nothing is dead or solid here in any way. It is mobile, fluid and full of life.

Bob: Have you passed through what Steiner called kamaloca, looking back on, or rather re-experiencing, your past life on Earth?

Ron: I have indeed, and I have learnt much by doing this. This is the reason why it is necessary to go back over one's last life and see what it has meant for others.

Bob: Will you reincarnate?

Ron: Yes I will, and then I will take on a new body and once again grow up as a child.

Bob: Do you know when that will be?

Ron: No, not yet. This is something that I must do together with the beings who are entrusted to guide human souls to their next incarnation on Earth.

Bob: I think that, for today, I have asked all the questions I can think of. Have you anything further you wish to say, father?

Ron: Let me simply say that it is a wonderful thing that you are able to make this contact with me. It is something which I have hoped for for a long time. You have a special gift, Robert, to be able to do this in the way that you do, and we hope that many others can benefit from your writings. All blessings, Dad.

Bob: Thank you.

(This was another 45 minute session.)

*

17th December 2019:

Bob: Father, I would like once again to link up with you in consciousness and to ask you real questions. By this I mean questions that are important for me to know the answers to, for my understanding of life in spirit worlds. Are you willing to work with me on this?

Ron: Robert, my son, I am more than willing to be of help to you and to do this work together. Please ask the questions which are important to you.

Bob: Right. Firstly, do you still have self-consciousness, father? Are you still aware of who you are?

Ron: Yes, my son, I am. I still have a sense for my self as a separate being and yet, at the same time, I can also merge myself with other beings, with other selves.

Bob: So, you have your own identity in spirit, is that correct?

Ron: Yes, it is. I am aware of myself and yet not restricted by myself, if that makes sense to you.

Bob: So, is this the same feeling, or sense of self, as you knew in your earthly life, or is it somehow a different sort of experience of self-hood?

Ron: It is different in the sense that it is wider, broader, more inclusive of others. This is what I meant by saying that it is not restrictive.

Bob: So, do you mean, for example, that you can have a closer, more intimate, relationship with others, with other souls, in the place where you now live?

Ron: Yes, it means precisely that. We are not separated in the same way as we were when living in the physical, material body.

Bob: What determines or influences how close you can get to another person in spirit?

Ron: It is purely a matter of what degree of love and affection lives between us. Where there is a strong tie of love, we are able to enter into the soul, the being, of the other person.

Bob: So, does the contrary also hold? Namely, that if there is no love between souls then they keep their distance?

Ron: Yes it does. If there is no loving link, then we are at a distance from each other. There is no penetration of soul within soul, in that case.

Bob: How is that with thinking? Can you think still?

Ron: Yes, I can think, but thinking is not abstract, it is a living force, a force of life in these worlds.

Bob: And what of feelings and emotions? Do you still experience these?

Ron: Yes, I do, but not in the sense that they are entirely personal. Rather, they have a life of their own and exist in the atmosphere around me.

Bob: What do you mean by 'atmosphere'?

Ron: I mean the soul substance, the soul texture, the quality of soul-life in which I live.

Bob: So this has to do with your soul environment?

Ron: Yes, precisely so. It has to do with the soul substance, the medium in which we live our lives here.

Bob: And what of will impulses? Are you able to exert your own will?

Ron: Again, I am, but at the same time I follow the laws of this land, so to speak. I fashion my will according to the requirements, the necessities, of the spirit world.

Bob: What does that mean then? Can you explain this further please?

Ron: Well, it is a matter of perceiving, of seeing, what needs to be done in order that the harmony of the world in which I live is not disrupted in any way. In other words, I act to live in accordance with the laws which belong to this realm of existence.

Bob: So, does this mean that you do not have freedom of will?

Ron: I do not have freedom of will in the sense that you believe you have freedom of will when in your earthly body. There is freedom to follow the laws of the divine order in which I now live.

Bob: But is this then freedom?

Ron: It is freedom in the context in which I live in spirit, but not freedom in the context in which you live in matter.

Bob: Are you happy in spirit, or are there difficulties or problems to deal with?

Ron: There are challenges to face up to. These are the challenges of gaining true self-knowledge, and in that sense these are not dissimilar to what you also face in your daily life on Earth.

Bob: So, do you now know who you are in your spirit being, your spirit reality?

Ron: Yes and no. I am on the way to this recognition and realisation. This is the purpose of the journey in spirit worlds – to eventually find oneself in actuality.

Bob: Do you have far to go to come to this realisation?

Ron: I do not know how far I have to go. I am still on this journey and I will find out where it will lead me to.

Bob: Are you alone on this journey, or are there others who are helping you?

Ron: We are never alone. We are helped and supported every step of the way. No one is left to fend for themselves. There is loving help at every turn.

Bob: Do you know my spirit guides, I mean Joshua, Dr John, and the others? Are they known to you?

Ron: Yes indeed, I am well aware of the guides who are working with you and who support you.

Bob: What of my guardian angel, Philip, are you also aware of him?

Ron: Yes, I am also aware of him as a being of light who watches over you.

Bob: Who else do you live with in spirit worlds?

Ron: I live with many people, many souls, who have a similar outlook to myself.

Bob: What does that mean, 'a similar outlook'?

Ron: It means that we have an affinity for each other, and that we can work together for the greater good of all.

Bob: How do you have an awareness of your surroundings?

Ron: I have an awareness because of my ability to enter into these different beings – yes, beings, really. It is a matter of feeling at one with what is around and also within myself.

Bob: Father, thank you. I am going to draw this session to a close. But first one more important question. Are you happy that I should include our conversations in my new book, or would you prefer that these remain only personal?

Ron: I am more than happy that you include all that we have said, if you feel that this would be of service to others. If it can help others to understand spirit worlds, then it is all to the good. All blessings, Dad.

Bob: Thank you, once again.

(This last session was 45 minutes.)

Reflections

I may continue to have further conversations with my father, perhaps with my mother also. We will see. However, for the purposes of this Appendix I have, with my father's permission, included those which took place on 13, 14, 15, 16 and 17 December 2019. As I pointed out before, if it had not been for my friend who had felt that 'concrete destiny' situations would be more interesting than generalities, I would never have thought to initiate these more personal conversations. Also, as I noted, they have taken place in exactly the same way, via telepathy, as the communications with my spirit guides. I am very grateful that this has been possible, as a cooperative, mutual and loving enquiry. Perhaps this will also give encouragement to others, to see how to develop their own links with friends in spirit?

As regards the content of the conversations, this seems to be confirmatory of what the guides shared with us previously. There were, however, some questions and answers from my father which shed further clarifications. For example, about his state of self-consciousness and identity in spirit worlds and his surroundings. There may of course be those readers who view what is contained in this book, including the Appendix, with some scepticism. This is, I think, not at all negative, if it serves as a stimulus for further questions and explorations of these areas of enquiry. After all, the fact of the matter is that eventually each and every one of us will die, as regards our physical life. What then follows we will, presumably, see for ourselves. However, it may well make a difference to this 'seeing' if beforehand we have done some serious preparations for 'our journey', as I explained in Chapters 2 and 3, with the analogy of making plans to travel to some foreign land. Through preparing ourselves, we may be better equipped to 'feel at home' in the Afterlife.

In conclusion, I would just like to quote the final words which my father wrote in his autobiography. He compiled this, at my suggestion, when aged 75. It gives a fascinating insight both into his own life and also the social and physical environments in which at various times he lived. This included the years of the Second World War, when he served in the RAF. Certainly it is a blessing to have such a family document, also containing many of his poems, to dip into and to reflect upon. In fact, he himself entitled it *Reflections*, and the closing words are, when he was referring to his and my mother's life together,

> We must still be fulfilling some purpose in this life, and we know that we will eventually reach the threshold of a new world as we pass over to a Higher Life.

In the light of everything in this book, I believe that his words do ring very true, at least to my mind.

AFTERWORD

In this book we have pursued a line of inquiry aimed at providing us with knowledge of higher, or spirit worlds, and of life after death. This research has been done by cooperating with those who live in these non-physical worlds, and who have acted as spirit guides for this specific purpose. Their communications have been received by me through a clear and conscious, direct telepathic transmission. The transparency of this allows for a flow of thoughts which can be written down verbatim, much in the same way as a good secretary accurately receives dictation. These spirit communications have been given freely in response to the questions asked and there is no room for any sort of coercion, imposition, manipulation or ulterior motives. Indeed, the pure intentionality of the process of telepathic interchange is essential to the validity and reliability of this fully conscious methodology. Therefore I have in no way edited, or otherwise altered, the communications as received directly from the guides. Nonetheless, as critical and perhaps sceptical enquirers we have to ask whether their replies are 'true'. Are they credible, believable and consistent, or do they leave us feeling doubtful and unconvinced? How can we test the substance of these alleged spirit communications?

As I proposed in the early chapters of this book we can, at least, make a modest comparative study with other acknowledged sources of spiritual research. However, given the very wide range of published material on spiritual themes available nowadays, a clear decision needed to be made for such referencing. In actual fact this was an easy choice for me to make, since my study of Rudolf Steiner's anthroposophy or spiritual science goes back fifty years. That being said, there is a huge amount of Steiner material to select from; at least 30 books and 6,000 lectures! Therefore, I have had to be quite judicious and circumspect in my references, for the purpose of composing the short 'Commentaries' for the guides' chapters. As I pointed out earlier, what I have provided as selected quotes from Steiner might, perhaps, be criticised as showing a distinct bias in support of my guides. To that possible accusation I can only say that I have tried to make a fair comparison. For example, whereas Steiner gives a clear description of the different regions or levels of the spirit worlds when speaking of what he refers to as 'the

Soul World' and 'the Country of Spirit Beings' in his book *Theosophy*, the guides do not provide us with the same systematic scenario. Or again, when the guides are addressing my questions about the length of time spent in spirit worlds after death and before we reincarnate on Earth, their answers may seem at odds with what Steiner says. However, here we should also bear in mind what may be described as the 'general' course or pattern of events, and how this generality may be modified and changed in the case of some individuals, for karmic reasons. This might then necessitate a much quicker reincarnation than is generally required for most people.

In spite of such seeming differences on some particular points, is there actually a good deal of common ground, agreements, between what the guides have given us and Steiner's own investigations? I believe it is fair to say that overall there is a good degree of correlation between these two independent research sources. Importantly, for those readers who wish to test this claim out further, I have made a point of giving clear references to the exact pages of all Steiner material I have referred to. Interestingly, in anthroposophy, Steiner himself often approaches a particular area of spiritual investigation from different vantage points. This very flexibility may sometimes lead readers to point to apparent contradictions in his statements. Steiner was well aware of such paradoxes. So, although we would all wish simply to have clear, unequivocal, factual knowledge of higher worlds, we also need to appreciate that we can approach the same theme from different angles. For example, whereas in *Theosophy* Steiner speaks of the journey through the spirit worlds in terms of passing through 'regions' or 'levels', elsewhere he refers to travelling through the various 'planetary spheres' after death. This is not at all contradictory, but comes at the same process from different perspectives, with one of them more cosmic than another. Still, as I made clear in Chapter 3, the purpose of this book is not to make out a case for Rudolf Steiner's findings *per se*, but rather to clearly present what my guides have presented us with.

It is of course in the nature of any serious research that it never really comes to an end. Rather, it is an ongoing process of inquiry, clarification, experimentation and reassessment. Moreover, whatever findings we may read about, it is still up to us as individuals to make up our own minds about what we are happy to take on board, given where we currently stand on our journey through life. Some things we may immediately say 'yes' to, whereas other matters may need to be put on the 'slow burner' for the time being, if not rejected outright. In truth, whether we consciously realise it or not, each of us carries his or her own philosophy, which consists not only of concepts, but also of moral and ethical values which provide our guiding stars. Our personal philosophy and values can of course change, grow and develop as we gain fresh experiences, ideas, assumptions, beliefs and encounters through life itself. I hope that what is contained in this book will contribute towards your own philosophy in a helpful, constructive and reassuring way; in particular, to know that death is very likely the door to a higher life in spirit worlds, in which our learning and evolution towards realising our true selves continues, for the benefit of ourselves and others.

In conclusion, I would simply like to say a great big 'thank you' to all the guides who have contributed to this book. Even after working with my guides for the past fifteen years, I still find it very remarkable that such conscious interchange between myself and friends in spirit can take place. Moreover, since I am convinced that each person has his or her own spirit guides, I would like to think that this book may also encourage others, *you* perhaps, to strike up your free communications with our close spirit friends. If this is done, then this link might well provide us with another, independent, source of confirmation for the contents given in the foregoing chapters. Researching, together with spirit, is truly an ongoing and inspiring journey of exploration and discovery. Our guides are ready to help us with this, when we are ready to request their help.

Postscript, 23 March 2020

The current global pandemic is having many serious repercussions for all our day-to-day lives. In a very real sense there are two pandemics that we have to deal with. One is the spread of the virus itself, while the other is the fear and uncertainty which it generates. These two diseases challenge us to reassess our own perspectives, values and priorities. Fundamentally, to become ever clearer about what is really most important to us. Surely this is, above all, our relationship to our loved ones, both family and friends. What the spirit guides have given us in this book is, I think, very reassuring under such difficult circumstances. Perhaps, when faced with existential problems, we are more open and awake to new, spiritual, perspectives? Certainly, our guides and angels stand ready to help us in every way they can. Ultimately, it is the transforming power of love which bridges all worlds and all beings.

All Blessings, Bob

A SELECT BIBILOGRAPHY

Alexander, E. and Newell, K. (2017) *Living in a Mindful Universe.* Piatkus

Alexander, E. with Tompkins, P. (2014) *The Map of Heaven.* Piatkus

Alexander, E. (2013) *Proof of Heaven.* Piatkus

Brink, M van den & Stolp, H. (2017) *What Happens When We Die. Our Journey in the Afterlife.* Temple Lodge

Greaves, H. (1969) *Testimony of Light.* World Fellowship Press Ltd.

Hawking, J. (2014) *Travelling To Infinity – My Life With Stephen.* Alma Books

Hogenboom, M. & Woodward, B. (2013) *Autism – A Holistic Approach.* Floris Books

Rovelli, C. (2016) *Reality Is Not What It Seems. The Journey to Quantum Gravity.* Allen Lane

Steiner, R. (1954) *From the Contents of the Esoteric School (Vol.III).* Anthroposophical Publishing Company

Steiner, R. (1959) *The Inner Nature of Man – And the Life between Death and a New Birth.* Anthroposophical Publishing Company

Steiner, R. (1963) *The Tension Between East and West.* Hodder and Stoughton

Steiner, R. (1969) *Knowledge of the Higher Worlds – How is it Achieved?* Rudolf Steiner Press

Steiner, R. (1970) *At the Gates of Spiritual Science.* Rudolf Steiner Press

Steiner, R. (1972a) *Karmic Relationships – Esoteric Studies, Vol.1.* Rudolf Steiner Press

Steiner, R. (1972b) *Christ and the Human Soul.* Rudolf Steiner Press

Steiner, R. (1975a) *Life between Death and Rebirth.* Anthroposophic Press

Steiner, R. (1975b) *Between Death and Rebirth.* Rudolf Steiner Press

Steiner, R. (1981) *Spiritual Research : Methods and Results.* Steinerbooks

Steiner, R. (1983) *The Spiritual Guidance of Man and Humanity.* Anthroposophic Press

Steiner, R. (1994) *Theosophy.* Anthroposophic Press

Steiner, R. (1995a) *Manifestations of Karma.* Rudolf Steiner Press

Steiner, R. (1995b) *Life Beyond Death.* Rudolf Steiner Press

Steiner, R. (1997) *An Outline of Esoteric Science.* Anthroposophic Press

Steiner, R. (1999a) *A Way of Self-Knowledge.* Anthroposophic Press

Steiner, R. (1999b) *Staying Connected – How to continue your relationship with those who have died.* Anthroposophic Press
Steiner, R. (2000) *Guardian Angels – Connecting with our Spiritual Guides and Helpers.* Rudolf Steiner Press
Van Praagh, J. (2017) *Wisdom from your Spirit Guides.* Hay House
Wetzl, J. (1974) *The Bridge Over the River.* Anthroposophic Press
White, R. & Swainson, M. (1971) *Gildas Communicates.* Neville Spearman
White R. (2004) *Working with Spirit Guides.* Piatkus
Woodward, B. (2018) *Trusting in Spirit – The Challenge.* Author House
Woodward, B. (2007) *Spirit Communications.* Athena Press
Woodward B. (2004) *Spirit Healing.* Floris Books
Woodward, B. (2007) *Spiritual Healing with Children with Special Needs.* Jessica Kingsley

ABOUT THE AUTHOR

I was born in 1947 in Gloucester, UK. At the age of eleven I had the good fortune to fail my 11-plus exam, which was then the entrance into secondary state education. Through this stroke of destiny, I entered Wynstones, an independent Rudolf Steiner School in Gloucestershire, where I remained for seven years until I was eighteen. Following 'A levels' in Maths and Physics I went to University and, a year later, became a university drop-out!

At the age of twenty-three, at Easter 1970, I was guided to become a co-worker at the Sheiling School in Thornbury, a centre of the Camphill Community, based on the teachings of Rudolf Steiner (1861-1925). Apart from a year at Emerson College in Sussex, I spent some forty years within the Camphill Movement, living with and teaching children with Special Educational Needs. I retired from this work in 2012.

I became a student of Steiner's Anthroposophy, having first read one of his fundamental books, *Knowledge of the Higher Worlds – How is it Achieved?* when I was around eighteen years old, now more than fifty years ago. Later I also became a member of the Anthroposophical Society in Great Britain. I have however always tried to keep an open-mind, and I consider myself a perpetual student. When I was forty-six I received an M.Ed degree from Bristol University and this was followed by an M.Phil when I was fifty. In 2011, I was awarded a Ph.D from the University of the West of England, when nearly sixty-four.

As well as being a qualified Curative Educator, I am also a spiritual healer and an author. I took a special interest in understanding autism in children and young people.

I have a lifelong interest in philosophy and spirituality, and in exploring the existential questions of life and death, meaning and freedom. Fundamentally, I see myself as a researcher in the field of spirituality, particularly in my conscious relationships with my spirit guides over the past fifteen years and my ongoing work with them.

In 2020 I will have been married for forty-two years, to Silke. We have five grown-up children and, currently, ten lively grandchildren. I enjoy walking, swimming, reading, writing, painting and tai chi. My wife and I particularly look forward to our holidays on the beautiful Isles of Scilly in Cornwall.

I feel that I have received clear guidance in my own life, and am very grateful for this.